THE PENGUIN POETS

D48

YET MORE COMIC AND
CURIOUS VERSE

YET MORE COMIC AND CURIOUS VERSE

COLLECTED BY

J. M. Cohen

PENGUIN BOOKS

Penguin Books Ltd, Harmondsworth, Middlesex
AUSTRALIA: Penguin Books Pty Ltd, 762 Whitehorse Road,
Mitcham, Victoria

First published 1959

—

Copyright © J. M. Cohen, 1959

Made and printed in Great Britain
by The Whitefriars Press Ltd
London and Tonbridge

To my son
David

Contents

Foreword

To produce a volume of *Yet More Comic and Curious Verse* might have been a difficult thing to do unaided. Since the appearance of *More Comic and Curious Verse* in 1956, a quantity of good material had come my way, but not enough, at the moment when I seriously began to collect again, to warrant a third volume. It occurred to me, however, to advertise in the Press for writers of suitable poems, and the response which I met was tremendous. It seems that the production of entertaining verse is almost a major industry in this country; the bottle-neck lies at the point of publication. Hardly any papers are prepared even to consider it. I have done my best to remedy this state of things slightly by including several writers quite unpublished, and to select pieces which have never appeared by writers who are lucky enough to have been printed.

The balance of this book, therefore, differs from that of the last two. Though I have found quite a few old poems that I had not met before and that deserve a place, and though I have raided *The Ingoldsby Legends*, as well as Hood and Calverley, for a piece or two, I have included chiefly living writers, or at least those not long dead. For these I have searched back-numbers of *Punch* and the *New Yorker*, and also the competition pages of the weeklies, and the dustier shelves of the London Library. In my searches I have had generous help from a number of friends known and unknown. Among these I must list Rachel Attwater, W. O. Baker, Anne Baxter, Douglas Browne, Stanley Buchan, Kenneth Budd, Miss Carew, Edmund Ford, Sir William Halliday, Brian Hill, John Irvine, Edmond Kapp, Allan M. Laing, Mrs E. Lardner, D. G. Leonard, J. A. Lindon, Ewart Milne, John Montgomery, John Parry, Eric Ratcliffe, Mrs Roberts, John Ross, W. Stark Toller, R. Tolson, B. B. Waddy, and Anthony Wilson; and I am particularly grateful to Captain Naish for his version of 'One Fish Ball', which I have never seen in print. Several of these friends are themselves contributors, who have introduced me to the work of others.

So the book grew over many months of searching and corre-spondence until I have come to think it as good as either of the earlier collections. Like them it is divided into sections, hortatory, instructive, and diverting. These I have named 'Moral Instruction', 'Unnatural History', 'The Sadness of Things', 'Unsocial Comment', 'A Clutch of Ballades', 'Words, Words, Words', 'Who'd be a Poet?' and 'Bits and Pieces'. In the antepenultimate section I have somewhat extended the bounds of nonsense to include such so-phisticated word-play as the macaronic, and in the last have put a variety of I-hope-not-unpleasing trifles, grouped together only for their brevity.

I owe no particular debts to any current anthology, but am, as usual, deeply indebted to members of my family – in this instance to my sons Mark and Philip – for help and criticism.

J.M.C.

Acknowledgements

FOR permission to reprint copyright matter, the following acknowledgements are made:

For four poems by W. Bridges Adams from *To Charlotte whilst Shaving*, to the author, Messrs James Barrie Ltd, and Messrs A. D. Peters; for four rhymes from *The Selected Letters of Hilaire Belloc* to Messrs Rupert Hart-Davis Ltd and Messrs A. D. Peters, and for one ballade by Belloc to Messrs A. D. Peters; for clerihews by the late E. C. Bentley to Mr Nicolas Bentley; for three poems by John Betjeman, one from *Continual Dew* and two from his *Collected Poems*, to the author and John Murray; for three poems by Morris Bishop to the Dial Press, New York; for one poem by Charles Causley from *Union Street* to the author and Messrs Rupert Hart-Davis; for a ballade by G. K. Chesterton from *101 Ballades*, to the executors of the author and Messrs A. P. Watt; for one poem by Patrick Galvin from *Heart of Grace* to the author and the Linden Press; for one poem by Daniel George from *Alphabetical Order* to the author and Messrs Jonathan Cape; for three *Bab Ballads* by Sir W. S. Gilbert, to the author's executors and Messrs Macmillan; for four *Ruthless Rhymes* by Harry Graham to the author's executors and Messrs Edwin Arnold Ltd, and for one poem from *Adam's Apples* to Messrs Methuen Ltd and A. P. Watt; for two poems by Robert Graves from *Collected Poems 1959* to the author and to Messrs Cassell and Co. Ltd, and Messrs A. P. Watt; for a speech from *Two Gentlemen of Soho* by Sir A. P. Herbert, to the author and Messrs Samuel French Ltd; for one poem by A. E. Housman to his literary executors, the Society of Authors; for one poem from *Leda* by Aldous Huxley to the author and Messrs Chatto and Windus Ltd; for one poem from *Oddly Boddlikins* and one from *Even Oddlier* by Paul Jennings, to the author and Messrs Max Reinhart Ltd; for three poems from *Stings and Honey* by L. E. Jones, to the author and Messrs Rupert Hart-Davis; for two poems by J. S. Kendall (Dum-dum) to Messrs Constable and Co. Ltd; for two poems from *The Poetical Works of Andrew Lang* to Messrs Longmans Green and Co. Ltd; for one poem by E. V. Lucas to Messrs Methuen and Co. Ltd; for one poem by E. McCurdy from *The Lays of a Limpet* to the Hutchinson Group (Messrs Selwyn Blount); for one poem from *The Love Letters of Phyllis McGinley* to Messrs J. M. Dent Ltd; for two ballades from *Ballades and other Verse* and *Rhyme and Reason* by W. S. Mackintosh to the author and Messrs Rupert Hart-Davis Ltd; for two poems from *Once More to Tourney* by Ewart Milne to the author and the Linden Press; for three poems from *Streamlines* by Christopher Morley to Messrs Faber and Faber Ltd; for three poems by J. B. Morton to the author and Messrs A. D. Peters; for twenty poems by Ogden Nash from *Family Reunion*, *You Can't Get There from Here*, and others of his books to Messrs J. M. Dent Ltd; for one poem from *A Shot in the Park* by

William Plomer to the author and Messrs Jonathan Cape Ltd; for a passage from *The Sweeniad* by Victor Purcell (Myra Buttle) to the author and Messrs Secker and Warburg Ltd; for a rhyme by Bernard Shaw to his literary executors, the Society of Authors; for two pieces from *Some Verse* by F. Sidgwick to Messrs Sidgwick and Jackson Ltd; for a piece by Evelyn Waugh to the author and Messrs A. D. Peters; and for four pieces by D. B. Wyndham Lewis to the author and Messrs A. D. Peters.

Further acknowledgements are due to the *New Yorker* for poems by Morris Bishop, R. Knowlton, David McCord, and Phyllis McGinley; and to the proprietors of *Punch* for poems by Peter Dickinson, Bernard Fergusson, Virginia Graham, Hans Hess, Brian Hill, K. Lillington, J. B. Naismith, J. Richardson, W. S. Slater, Stevie Smith, Richard Usborne, and G. H. Vallins. Other copyright material includes two winning entries to competitions in the *New Statesman* by D. R. Peddy and F. Sinclair, and one in the *Spectator* by H. A. C. Evans, and a considerable number of poems that make their first appearance in this book. Several authors remain untraced, and to them apologies are offered.

J. M. C.

MORAL INSTRUCTION

The Nobleman

A noble lord once passed away –
A debt all noble lords must pay,
    Although they find this world delightful.
    And that is frightful,
    To die, when life is so delightful.

The noble lord my tale's about,
Poor wretch, when Death had sought him out,
    Came where you try in vain to freeze.
    And that's hard cheese,
    When people try in vain to freeze.

He met his coachman, and a yell
Escaped him: 'What! John too in Hell?
    I hardly can believe my eyes' –
    And that's unwise,
    To see, and disbelieve your eyes.

'The reason why I'm in this mess
I'm loth to tell you, though I guess
    You know too well the full particulars' –
    And that's ridiculous,
    To try to hide well-known particulars.

'My son spent such a pile on dice,
Women, and other kinds of vice,
    He drained the pockets of his dad' –
    And that is bad,
    To drain the pockets of your dad.

'To help that precious rascal, I
Confess I squeezed my tenants dry,

And turned a deaf ear to their wailing' –
And that's a failing,
To disregard your tenants' wailing.

'But you, who were so very pi,
And wouldn't even hurt a fly,
To know why *you* are here, I'm curious' –
And that's injurious,
Always to be so very curious.

'I'm here', said John, 'because of one
Success I had where you had none,
Although you did your level best' –
And that's a pest,
To fail when you have done your best.

'That son, for whom you've earned damnation,
I grieve to say, was my creation.
The lady's wish was not deniable' –
And that's too pliable,
To find no lady's wish deniable.

The moral for a lively lad is:
Never to make your neighbours daddies,
Not if their wives are quite importunate.
And that's unfortunate,
When neighbours' wives are quite importunate.

JOHAN HERMAN WESSEL
(translated by O. G. W. STALLYBRASS)

The Pilgrims and the Peas

A TRUE STORY

A brace of Sinners, for no good,
    Were ordered to the Virgin Mary's shrine,
Who at Loreto dwelt, in Wax, Stone, Wood,
    And in a fair white Wig looked wondrous fine.

Fifty long miles had those sad Rogues to travel,
With something in their shoes much worse than gravel:
In short, their toes so gentle to amuse,
The Priest had ordered *peas* into their shoes;

A nostrum famous in old Popish times,
For purifying souls that stunk of crimes;
    A sort of Apostolic *salt*,
    Which Popish parsons for its powers exalt,
For keeping Souls of Sinners *sweet*,
Just as our Kitchen-salt keeps meat.

The Knaves set off on the same day,
Peas in their shoes, to go and pray;
    But very different was their speed, I wot:
One of the Sinners galloped on,
Swift as a Bullet from a gun;
    The other limped as if he had been shot.

One saw the Virgin soon; *peccavi* cried;
    Had his Soul whitewashed all so clever;
Then home again he nimbly hied,
    Made fit with Saints above to live for ever.

In coming back, however, let me say,
He met his Brother-rogue about half-way,
Hobbling with ... bended knees,
Damning the *souls* and *bodies* of the *peas;*
His eyes in tears, his cheeks and brows in sweat,
Deep sympathizing with his groaning feet.

'How now,' the light-toed, white-washed Pilgrim broke
    'You lazy lubber?'
'Odds curse it,' cried the other, ''tis no joke‧
My Feet, once hard as any Rock,
    Are now as soft as Blubber.

'Excuse me, Virgin Mary, that I swear;
As for Loreto, I shall not get there;
No, to the Devil my sinful soul must go,
For damme if I ha'nt lost every toe.

'But, Brother-sinner, pray explain
How 'tis that *you* are not in pain;
   What Power hath worked a wonder for *your* toes;
Whilst *I* just like a Snail am crawling,
Now swearing, now on Saints devoutly bawling,
   While not a rascal comes to ease my woes?

'How is't that *you* can like a Greyhound go,
Merry as if that nought had happened, burn ye?' –
'Why', cried the other grinning, 'you must know,
That just before I ventured on my journey,
   To walk a little more at ease,
   I *took the liberty* to boil *my* Peas.'

JOHN WOLCOT (PETER PINDAR)

Lodgings for Single Gentlemen

Who has e'er been in London, that overgrown place,
Has seen 'Lodgings to Let' stare him full in the face:
Some are good, and let dearly; while some, 'tis well known,
Are so dear, and so bad, they are best let alone.

Will Waddle, whose temper was studious and lonely,
Hired lodgings that took Single Gentlemen only;
But Will was so fat he appeared like a ton –
Or like two Single Gentlemen rolled into one.

He entered his rooms, and to bed he retreated;
But, all the night long, he felt fevered and heated;
And, though heavy to weigh as a score of fat sheep,
He was not, by any means, heavy to sleep.

Next night, 'twas the same! – and the next; and the next;
He perspired like an ox; he was nervous, and vexed;
Week passed after week; till, by weekly succession,
His weakly condition was past all expression.

In six months his acquaintance began much to doubt him;
For his skin, 'like a lady's loose gown', hung about him.
He sent for a doctor; and cried, like a ninny,
'I have lost many pounds – make me well – there's a guinea.'

The doctor looked wise: – 'a slow fever', he said:
Prescribed sudorifics, – and going to bed.
'Sudorifics in bed', exclaimed Will, 'are humbugs!
I've enough of them there, without paying for drugs!'

Will kicked out the doctor: – but, when ill indeed,
E'en dismissing the doctor don't *always* succeed;
So, calling his host – he said – 'Sir, do you know,
I'm the fat Single Gentleman, six months ago?

'Look'e, landlord, I think,' argued Will with a grin,
'That with honest intentions you first *took me in:*
But from the first night – and to say it I'm bold –
I have been so damned hot that I'm sure I caught cold.'

Quoth the landlord – 'Till now I ne'er had a dispute;
I've let lodgings ten years – I'm a baker to boot;
In airing your sheets, sir, my wife is no sloven;
And your bed is immediately – over my oven.'

'The oven ! ! !' says Will. Says the host, 'Why this passion?
In that excellent bed died three people of fashion.

'Why so crusty, good sir?' – 'Zounds!' cries Will in a taking,
'Who wouldn't be crusty with half a year's baking?'

Will paid for his rooms. Cried the host with a sneer,
'Well, I see you've been *going away* half a year.'
'Friend, we can't well agree – yet not quarrel' – Will said:
'But I'd rather not *perish* while you *make your bread*.'

GEORGE COLMAN, THE YOUNGER

The Lay of St Cuthbert

OR

The Devil's Dinner-Party

(A LEGEND OF THE NORTH COUNTREE)

It's in Bolton Hall, and the clock strikes One,
And the roast meat's brown and the boil'd meat's done,
And the barbecu'd sucking-pig's crisp'd to a turn,
And the pancakes are fried, and beginning to burn;
       The fat stubble-goose
       Swims in gravy and juice,
With the mustard and apple-sauce ready for use;
Fish, flesh, and fowl, and all of the best,
Want nothing but eating – they're all ready drest,
But where is the Host, and where is the Guest?

Pantler and serving-man, henchman and page,
Stand sniffing the duck-stuffing (onion and sage),
       And the scullions and cooks,
       With fidgety looks,
Are grumbling and mutt'ring, and scowling as black
As cooks always do when the dinner's put back;
For though the board's deckt, and the napery, fair
As the unsunn'd snow-flake, is spread out with care,

And the Dais is furnish'd with stool and with chair,
And plate of *orfèvrerie* costly and rare,
Apostle-spoons, salt-cellar, all are there,
    And Mess John in his place,
    With his rubicund face,
And his hands ready folded, prepared to say Grace,
Yet where is the Host? – and his convives – where?

The Scroope sits lonely in Bolton Hall,
And he watches the dial that hangs by the wall,
He watches the large hand, he watches the small,
    And he fidgets and looks
    As cross as the cooks,
And he utters – a word which we'll soften to 'Zooks!'
And he cries, 'What on earth has become of them all?' –
    What can delay
    De Vaux and De Saye?
What makes Sir Gilbert de Umfraville stay?
What's gone with Poyntz, and Sir Reginald Braye?
Why are Ralph Ufford and Marny away?
And De Nokes, and De Styles, and Lord Marmaduke Grey?
    And De Roe?
    And De Doe? –
Poynings, and Vavasour – where be they?
Fitz-Walter, Fitz-Osbert, Fitz-Hugh, and Fitz-John,
And the Mandevilles, *père et filz* (father and son)?
Their cards said 'Dinner precisely at One!'
    There's nothing I hate, in
    The world, like waiting!
It's a monstrous great bore, when a Gentleman feels
A good appetite, thus to be kept from his meals!'

It's in Bolton Hall, and the clock strikes Two!
And the scullions and cooks are themselves in 'a stew',
And the kitchen-maids stand, and don't know what to do,
For the rich plum-puddings are bursting their bags,
And the mutton and turnips are boiling to rags,

And the fish is all spoil'd,
And the butter's all oil'd,
And the soup's got cold in the silver tureen,
And there's nothing, in short, that is fit to be seen!
While Sir Guy Le Scroope continues to fume,
And to fret by himself in the tapestried room,
And still fidgets, and looks
More cross than the cooks,
And repeats that bad word, which we've soften'd to 'Zooks!'

Two o'clock's come, and Two o'clock's gone,
And the large and the small hands move steadily on,
Still nobody's there,
No De Roes, or De Clare,
To taste of the Scroope's most delicate fare,
Or to quaff off a health unto Bolton's Heir,
That nice little boy who sits there in his chair,
Some four years old, and a few months to spare,
With his laughing blue eyes, and his long curly hair,
Now sucking his thumb, and now munching his pear.

Again, Sir Guy the silence broke,
'It's hard upon Three! – it's just on the stroke!
Come, serve up the dinner! – A joke is a joke!' –
Little he deems that Stephen de Hoaques,
Who 'his fun' as the Yankees say, everywhere 'pokes',
And is always a great deal too fond of his jokes,
Has written a circular note to De Nokes,
And De Stiles, and De Roe, and the rest of the folks,
One and all,
Great and small,
Who were asked to the Hall
To dine there and sup, and wind up with a ball,
And had told all the party a great bouncing lie, he
Cook'd up, that 'the *fête* was postponed *sine die*,
The dear little curly-wig'd heir of Le Scroope,
Being taken alarmingly ill with the croup!'

When the clock struck Three,
And the Page on his knee
Said 'An't please you, Sir Guy Le Scroope, *On a servi!*'
And the Knight found the banquet-hall empty and clear,
With nobody near
To partake of his cheer.
He stamp'd, and he storm'd – then his language! – Oh dear!
'Twas awful to see, and 'twas awful to hear!
And he cried to the button-deck'd Page at his knee,
Who had told him so civilly '*On a servi,*'
'Ten thousand fiends seize them, wherever they be!
– The Devil take *them!* and the Devil take *thee!*
And the DEVIL MAY EAT UP THE DINNER FOR ME! !'

In a terrible fume
He bounced out of the room,
He bounced out of the house – and page, footman, and groom,
Bounced after their master; for scarce had they heard
Of this left-handed Grace the last finishing word,
Ere the horn at the gate of the Barbican tower
Was blown with a loud twenty-trumpeter power,
And in rush'd a troop
Of strange guests! – such a group
As had ne'er before darken'd the door of the Scroope!

This looks like De Saye – yet – it is not De Saye –
And this is – no, 'tis not – Sir Reginald Braye –
This has somewhat the favour of Marmaduke Grey –
But stay! – *Where on earth did he get those long nails?*
Why, they're *claws!* – then Good Gracious! – they've all of them
tails?
That can't be De Vaux – why his nose is a bill,
Or, I would say a beak! – and he can't keep it still! –
Is that Poynings? – Oh Gemini! – look at his feet! !
Why, they're absolute *hoofs!* – is it gout or his corns
That have crumpled them up so? – by jingo, he's *horns!*

Run! run! – There's Fitz-Walter, Fitz-Hugh, and Fitz-John,
And the Mandevilles, *père et filz* (father and son),
And Fitz-Osbert, and Ufford – *they've all got them on!*
          Then their great saucer eyes –
          It's the Father of lies
And his Imps – run! run! run! – they're all fiends in disguise,
Who've partly assumed, with more sombre complexions,
The forms of Sir Guy Le Scroope's friends and connexions,
And He – at the top there – that grim-looking elf –
Run! run! – that's the 'muckle-horned Clootie' himself!

          And now what a din
          Without and within!
For the court-yard is full of them. – How they begin
To mop, and to mowe, and make faces, and grin!
          Cock their tails up together,
          Like cows in hot weather,
And butt at each other, all eating and drinking,
The viands and wine disappearing like winking.
          And then such a lot
          As together had got!
Master Cabbage, the steward, who'd made a machine
To calculate with, and count noses, – I ween
The cleverest thing of the kind ever seen, –
          Declared, when he'd made,
          By the said machine's aid,
Up, what's now called, the 'tottle' of those he survey'd,
There were just – how he proved it I cannot divine, –
Nine thousand, nine hundred, and ninety, and nine.
          Exclusive of Him
          Who, giant in limb,
And black as the crow they denominate *Jim*,
With a tail like a bull, and a head like a bear,
Stands forth at the window, – and what holds he there,
          Which he hugs with such care,
          And pokes out in the air,

And grasps as its limbs from each other he'd tear?
                    Oh! grief and despair!
                    I vow and declare
It's Le Scroope's poor, dear, sweet, little, curly-wig'd Heir!
Whom the nurse had forgot, and left there in his chair,
Alternately sucking his thumb and his pear!

                    What words can express
                    The dismay and distress
Of Sir Guy, when he found what a terrible mess
His cursing and banning had now got him into?
That words, which to use are a shame and a sin too,
Had thus on their speaker recoil'd, and his malison
Placed in the hands of the Devil's own 'pal' his son! –
                    He sobb'd and he sigh'd,
                    And he scream'd, and he cried,
And behaved like a man that is mad, or in liquor, – he
Tore his peak'ed beard, and he dash'd off his 'Vicary',
                    Stamped on the jasey
                    As though he were crazy,

And staggering about just as if he were 'hazy',
Exclaimed, 'Fifty pounds!' (a large sum in those times)
'To the person, whoever he may be, that climbs
To that window above there, *en ogive*, and painted,
And bring down my curly-wi' – ' here Sir Guy fainted!

                    With many a moan,
                    And many a groan,
What with tweaks of the nose, and some *eau-de-Cologne*,
He revived, – Reason once more remounted her throne,
Or rather the instinct of Nature, – 'twere treason
To Her, in the Scroope's case, perhaps, to say Reason, –
But what saw he then? – Oh! my goodness! a sight
Enough to have banished his reason outright! –

In that broad banquet hall
The fiends one and all,
Regardless of shriek, and of squeak, and of squall,
From one to another were tossing that small
Pretty, curly-wig'd boy, as if playing at ball:
Yet none of his friends or his vassals might dare
To fly to the rescue, or rush up the stair,
And bring down in safety his curly-wig'd Heir!

Well a day! Well a day!
All he can say
Is but just so much trouble and time thrown away;
Not a man can be tempted to join the *mêlée*,
E'en those words cabalistic, 'I promise to pay
Fifty pounds on demand,' have, for once, lost their sway,
And there the Knight stands,
Wringing his hands
In his agony – when on a sudden, one ray
Of hope darts through his midriff! – His Saint! – Oh, it's funny,
And almost absurd,
That it never occurr'ed! –
'Ay! the Scroope's Patron Saint! – he's the man for my money.
Saint – who is it? – really, I'm sadly to blame, –
On my word I'm afraid, – I confess it with shame, –
That I've almost forgot the good Gentleman's name, –
Cut – let me see – Cutbeard? – no! – CUTHBERT! – egad
St Cuthbert of Bolton! – I'm right – he's the lad!
Oh, holy St Cuthbert, if forbears of mine –
Of myself I say little, – have knelt at your shrine,
And have lashed their bare backs, and – no matter – with twine,
Oh! list to the vow
Which I make to you now,
Only snatch my poor little boy out of the row
Which that Imp's kicking up with his fiendish bow-wow,
And his head like a bear, and his tail like a cow!
Bring him back here in safety! – perform but this task,

And I'll give! – Oh! – I'll give you whatever you ask! –
          There is not a shrine
          In the County shall shine
With a brilliancy half so resplendent as thine,
Or have so many candles, or look half so fine! –
Haste, holy St Cuthbert, then, – hasten in pity!' –
       – Conceive his surprise
       When a strange voice replies,
'It's a bargain! – but, mind, sir, THE BEST SPERMACETI!' –
Say, whose that voice? – whose that form by his side,
That old, old, grey man, with his beard long and wide,
       In his coarse Palmer's weeds,
       And his cockle and beads? –
And, how did he come? – did he walk? – did he ride?
Oh! none could determine, – oh! none could decide, –
The fact is, I don't believe any one tried,
For while ev'ry one stared, with a dignified stride,
       And without a word more,
       He march'd on before,
Up a flight of stone steps, and so through the front door,
To the banquetting-hall, that was on the first floor,
While the fiendish assembly were making a rare
Little shuttlecock there of the curly-wig'd Heir. –
– I wish, gentle Reader, that you could have seen
The pause that ensued when he stepp'd in between,
With his resolute air, and his dignified mien,
And said, in a tone most decided, though mild,
'Come! – I'll trouble you just to hand over that child!'

       The Demoniac crowd
       In an instant seem'd cowed;
Not one of the crew volunteer'd a reply,
All shrunk from the glance of that keen-flashing eye,
Save one horrid Humgruffin, who seem'd by his talk,
And the airs he assumed, to be Cock of the walk,
He quailed not before it, but saucily met it,

And as saucily said, 'Don't you wish you may get it?'
My goodness! – the look that the old Palmer gave!
And his frown! – 'twas quite dreadful to witness – 'Why, slave!
        You rascal!' quoth he,
          'This language to ME!!
– At once, Mr Nicholas! down on your knee,
And hand me that curly-wig'd boy! – I command it –
Come! – none of your nonsense! – you know I won't stand it.'

Old Nicholas trembled, – he shook in his shoes,
And seem'd half inclined, but afraid, to refuse.
        'Well, Cuthbert,' said he,
          'If so it must be,
– For you've had your own way from the first time I knew ye; –
Take your curly-wig'd brat, and much good may he do ye!
But I'll have in exchange –' – here his eye flash'd with rage –
'That chap with the buttons – he *gave me* the Page!'

'Come, come,' the Saint answer'd, 'you very well know
The young man's no more his than your own to bestow –
Touch one button of his if you dare, Nick – no! no!
Cut your stick, sir – come, mizzle! – be off with you! – go!' –
        The Devil grew hot –
        'If I do I'll be shot!
An you come to that, Cuthbert, I'll tell you what's what;
He has *asked* us to *dine here*, and go we will not!
        Why you Skinflint, – at least
        You may leave us the feast!
Here we've come all that way from our brimstone abode,
Ten million good leagues, Sir, as ever you strode,
And the deuce of a luncheon we've had on the road –
– "Go!" – "Mizzle!" indeed – Mr Saint, who are you,
I should like to know? – "Go!" – I'll be hanged if I do!
He invited us all – we've a right here – it's known
That a Baron may do what he likes with his own –
Here, Asmodeus – a slice of that beef; – now the mustard! –

What have *you* got? – oh, apple-pie – try it with custard!'
        The Saint made a pause
        As uncertain, because
He knew Nick is pretty well 'up' in the laws,
And they *might* be on *his* side – and then, he'd such claws!
On the whole, it was better, he thought, to retire
With the curly-wig'd boy he'd pick'd out of the fire,
And give up the victuals – to retrace his path,
And to compromise – (spite of the Member for Bath).
        So to Old Nick's appeal,
        As he turn'd on his heel,
He replied, 'Well, I'll leave you the mutton and veal,
And the soup *à la Reine*, and the sauce *Béchamel;*
As The Scroope *did* invite you to dinner, I feel
I can't well turn you out – 'twould be hardly genteel –
But be moderate, pray, – and remember thus much,
Since you're treated as Gentlemen, show yourselves such,
        And don't make it late,
        But mind and go straight
Home to bed when you've finished – and don't steal the plate!
Nor wrench off the knocker, or bell from the gate.
Walk away, like respectable Devils, in peace,
And don't "lark" with the watch, or annoy the police!'

        Having thus said his say,
        That Palmer grey
Took up little Le Scroope, and walk'd coolly away,
While the Demons all set up a 'Hip! hip! hurray!'
Then fell, tooth and claw, on the victuals, as they
Had been guests at Guildhall upon Lord Mayor's day,
All scrambling and scuffling for what was before 'em,
No care for precedence or common decorum.
        Few ate more hearty
        Than Madame Astarte,
And Hecate, – considered the Belles of the party.
Between them was seated Leviathan, eager

To 'do the polite', and take wine with Belphegor;
Here was *Morbleu* (a French devil), supping soup-meagre,
And there, munching leeks, Davy Jones of Tredegar
(A Welsh one), who'd left the domains of Ap Morgan,
To 'follow the sea', – and next him Demogorgon, –
Then Pan with his pipes, and Fauns grinding the organ
To Mammon and Belial, and half a score dancers,
Who'd joined with Medusa to get up 'the Lancers';
– Here's Lucifer lying blind drunk with Scotch ale,
While Beëlzebub's tying huge knots in his tail.
There's Setebos, storming because Mephistopheles
    Gave him the lie,
     Said he'd 'blacken his eye',
And dash'd in his face a whole cup of hot coffee-lees; –
    Ramping, and roaring,
     Hiccoughing, snoring,
Never was seen such a riot before in‾
A gentleman's house, or such profligate revelling
At any *soirée* – where they don't let the Devil in.

     Hark! – as sure as fate
     The clock's striking Eight!
(An hour which our ancestors called 'getting late'),
When Nick, who by this time was rather elate,
Rose up and addressed them.
 ''Tis full time,' he said,
'For all elderly Devils to be in their bed;
For my own part I mean to be jogging, because
I don't find myself now quite so young as I was;
But, Gentlemen, ere I depart from my post,
I must call on you all for one bumper – the toast
Which I have to propose is – OUR EXCELLENT HOST!
– Many thanks for his kind hospitality – may
    We also be able,
    To see at *our* table

Himself, and enjoy, in a family way,
His good company *down stairs* at no distant day!
            You'd
        I'm sure, think me rude
        If I did not include
In the toast my young friend there, the curly-wig'd Heir!
He's in very good hands, for you're all well aware
That St Cuthbert has taken him under his care;
        Though I must not say "bless", –
        – Why you'll easily guess, –
May our curly-wig'd Friend's shadow never be less!'
Nick took off his heel-taps – bow'd – smiled – with an air
Most graciously grim – and vacated the chair, –
        Of course the *élite*
        Rose at once on their feet,
And followed their leader, and beat a retreat;
When a sky-larking Imp took the President's seat,
And, requesting that each would replenish his cup,
Said, 'Where we have dined, my boys, there let us sup!' –
– It was three in the morning before they broke up!!!

*

        I scarcely need say
        Sir Guy didn't delay
To fulfil his vow made to St Cuthbert, or pay
For the candles he'd promised, or make light as day
The shrine he assured him he'd render so gay.
In fact, when the votaries came there to pray,
All said there was nought to compare with it – nay,
        For fear that the Abbey
        Might think he was shabby,
Four Brethren thenceforward, two cleric, two lay,
He ordained should take charge of a new-founded chantry,
With six marcs apiece, and some claims on the pantry;
        In short, the whole County
        Declared, through his bounty,

The Abbey of Bolton exhibited fresh scenes
From any displayed since Sir William de Meschines,
And Cecily Roumeli came to this nation
With William the Norman, and laid its foundation.

For the rest, it is said,
And I know I have read
In some Chronicle – whose, has gone out of my head –
That, what with these candles, and other expenses,
Which no man would go to if quite in his senses,
He reduced, and brought low
His property so,
That, at last, he'd not much of it left to bestow;
And that, many years after that terrible feast,
Sir Guy, in the Abbey, was living a Priest;
And there, in one thousand and – something, – deceased.
(It's supposed by this trick
He bamboozled Old Nick,
And slipped through his fingers remarkably 'slick'.)
While, as to young Curly-wig, – dear little Soul,
Would you know more of him, you must look at 'The Roll',
Which records the dispute,
And the subsequent suit,
Commenced in 'Thirteen sev'nty-five', – which took root
In Le Grosvenor's assuming the arms Le Scroope swore
That none but *his* ancestors, ever before,
In foray, joust, battle, or tournament wore,
To wit, '*On a Prussian-blue Field, a Bend Or;*'
While the Grosvenor averred that *his* ancestor bore
The same, and Scroope lied like a – somebody tore
Off the simile – so I can tell you no more,
Till some A double S shall the fragment restore.

MORAL

This Legend sound maxims exemplifies – *e.g.*

1*mo.*   Should any thing tease you,
                         Annoy, or displease you,
       Remember what Lilly says, '*Animum rege!*'
       And as for that shocking bad habit of swearing –
       In all good society voted past bearing –
       Eschew it! and leave it to dustmen and mobs,
       Nor commit yourself much beyond 'Zooks!' or 'Odsbobs!'

2*do.*   When asked out to dine by a Person of Quality,
         Mind, and observe the most strict punctuality!
                         For should you come late,
                         And make dinner wait,
         And the victuals get cold, you'll incur, sure as fate,
         The Master's displeasure, the Mistress's hate.
         And – though both may, perhaps, be too well-bred to swear, –
         They'll heartily *wish* you – I need not say *Where*.

3*tio.* Look well to your Maid-servants! – say you expect them
         To see to the children, and not to neglect them!
         And if you're a widower, just throw a cursory
         Glance in, at times, when you go near the Nursery.
         – Perhaps it's as well to keep children from plums,
         And from pears in the season, – and sucking their thumbs!

4*to.*   To sum up the whole with a 'Saw' of much use,
         Be *just* and be *generous*, – don't be *profuse!* –
         Pay the debts that you owe, – keep your word to your
                 friends,
         But – D O N ' T   S E T   Y O U R   C A N D L E S   A L I G H T   A T
                 B O T H   E N D S !! –

For of this be assured, if you 'go it' too fast,
    You'll be 'dish'd' like Sir Guy,
    And like him, perhaps, die
A poor, old, half-starved, Country Parson at last!

R. H. BARHAM

A Bow Street Ballad

BY A GENTLEMAN OF THE FORCE

There's in the Vest a city pleasant,
    To vich KING BLADUD gev his name,
And in that city there's a Crescent,
    Vere dwelt a noble knight of fame.

Although that galiant knight is oldish,
    Although SIR JOHN as grey, grey air,
Hage has not made his busum coldish,
    His Art still beats tewodds the Fair!

'Twas two years sins, this knight so splendid,
    Peraps fateagued with's Bath's routines,
To Paris towne his phootsteps bended
    In sutch of gayer folks and seans.

His and was free, his means was easy,
    A nobler, finer gent than he
Ne'er drove about the Shons-Eleesy,
    Or paced the Roo de rivolee.

A brougham and pair SIR JOHN prowided,
    In which abroad he loved to ride;
But ar! he most of all enjoy'd it,
    When some one helse was sittin' inside!

That 'some one helse' a lovely dame was,
  Dear ladies, you will heasy tell –
COUNTESS GRABROWSKI her sweet name was,
  A nobler title, ard to spell.

This faymus COUNTESS ad a daughter
  Of lovely form and tender art;
A nobleman in marriage sought her,
  By name the BARON OF SAINT BART.

Their pashn touched the noble SIR JOHN,
  It was so pewer and profound;
LADY GRABROWSKI he did urge on,
  With Hyming's wreath their loves to crownd.

'O, come to Bath, to Lansdowne Crescent,'
  Says kind SIR JOHN, 'and live with me;
The living there's uncommon pleasant –
  I'm sure you'll find the hair agree.

'O, come to Bath, my fair GRABROWSKI,
  And bring your charming girl,' sezee;
'The BARRING here shall have the ouse-key,
  Vith breakfast, dinner, lunch, and tea.

'And when they've passed an appy winter,
  Their opes and loves no more we'll bar;
The marridge-vow they'll enter inter,
  And I at Church will be their Par.'

To Bath they went to Lansdowne Crescent,
  Where good SIR JOHN he did provide
No end of teas, and balls incessant,
  And hosses both to drive and ride.

He was so Ospitably busy,
　　When Miss was late, he'd make so bold
Upstairs to call out, 'Missy, Missy,
　　Come down, the coffy's getting cold!'

But O! 'tis sadd to think such bounties
　　Should meet with such return as this;
O, BARRING OF SAINT BART, O COUNTESS
　　GRABROWSKI, and O, cruel Miss!

He married you at Bath's fair Habby,
　　SAINT BART he treated like a son –
And wasn't it uncommon shabby
　　To do what you have went and done!

My trembling And amost refewses
　　To write the charge which SIR JOHN swore
Of which the COUNTESS he ecuses,
　　Her daughter and her son-in-lore.

My Mews quite blushes as she sings of
　　The fatle charge which now I quote:
He says Miss took his two best rings off,
　　And pawned 'em for a tenpun note.

'Is this the child of honest parince,
　　To make a way with folks' best things?
Is this, pray, like the wives of BARRINS,
　　To go and prig a gentleman's rings?'

Thus thought SIR JOHN, by anger wrought on,
　　And to rewenge his injured cause,
He brought them hup to Mr Broughton,
　　Last Vensday veek as ever waws.

If guiltless, how she have been slanderd!
  If guilty, wengeance will not fail;
Meanwhile, the lady is remanderd
  And gev three hundred pounds in bail.

                              W. M. THACKERAY

My Familiar

'ECCE ITERUM CRISPINUS!'

Again I hear that creaking step! –
  He's rapping at the door! –
Too well I know the boding sound
  That ushers in a bore.
I do not tremble when I meet
  The stoutest of my foes,
But Heaven defend me from the Friend
  Who comes – but never goes!

He drops into my easy-chair,
  And asks about the news;
He peers into my manuscript,
  And gives his candid views;
He tells me where he likes the line,
  And where he's forced to grieve;
He takes the strangest liberties, –
  But never takes his leave!

He reads my daily paper through
  Before I've seen a word;
He scans the lyric (that I wrote)
  And thinks it quite absurd;
He calmly smokes my last cigar,
  And coolly asks for more;
He opens everything he sees –
  Except the entry door!

He talks about his fragile health,
    And tells me of the pains
He suffers from a score of ills
    Of which he ne'er complains;
And how he struggled once with death
    To keep the fiend at bay;
On themes like those away he goes, –
    But never goes away!

He tells me of the carping words
    Some shallow critic wrote;
And every precious paragraph
    Familiarly can quote;
He thinks the writer did me wrong;
    He'd like to run him through!
He says a thousand pleasant things, –
    But never says, 'Adieu!'

Whene'er he comes, – that dreadful man, –
    Disguise it as I may,
I know that, like an Autumn rain,
    He'll last throughout the day.
In vain I speak of urgent tasks;
    In vain I scowl and pout;
A frown is no extinguisher, –
    It does not put him out!

I mean to take the knocker off,
    Put crape upon the door,
Or hint to John that I am gone
    To stay a month or more.
I do not tremble when I meet
    The stoutest of my foes,
But Heaven defend me from the friend
    Who never, never goes!

J. G. SAXE

Don't Ask For Bread

A wretched man walked up and down
To buy his dinner in the town.

At last he found a wretched place
And entered in with modest grace,

Took off his coat, took off his hat,
And wiped his feet upon the mat,

Took out his purse to count his pence
And found he had but two half-cents.

The bill of fare, he scanned it through
To see what two half-cents would do.

The only item of them all
For two half-cents was one fishball.

So to the waiter he did call
And gently whispered: One fishball.

The waiter bellowed down the hall;
This gentleman here wants one fishball.

The diners looked both one and all
To see who wanted one fishball.

The wretched man, all ill at ease
Said: A little bread, sir, if you please.

The waiter bellowed down the hall:
We don't serve bread with one fishball.

The wretched man, he felt so small,
He quickly left the dining hall.

The wretched man, he went outside
And shot himself until he died.

This is the moral of it all,
Don't ask for bread with one fishball.

ANON.

The Reverend Simon Magus

A rich advowson, highly prized,
For private sale was advertised;
And many a parson made a bid;
The Reverend Simon Magus did.

He sought the agent's: 'Agent, I
Have come prepared at once to buy
(If your demand is not too big)
The Cure of Otium-cum-Digge.'

'Ah!' said the agent, '*there's* a berth –
The snuggest vicarage on earth;
No sort of duty (so I hear),
And fifteen hundred pounds a year!

'If on the price we should agree,
The living soon will vacant be;
The good incumbent's ninety-five,
And cannot very long survive.

'See – here's his photograph – you see,
He's in his dotage.' 'Ah, dear me!

Poor soul!' said Simon. 'His decease
Would be a merciful release!'

The agent laughed – the agent blinked –
The agent blew his nose and winked
And poked the parson's ribs in play –
It was that agent's vulgar way.

The Reverend Simon frowned: 'I grieve
This light demeanour to perceive;
It's scarcely *comme il faut*, I think:
Now – pray oblige me – do not wink.

'Don't dig my waistcoat into holes –
Your mission is to sell the souls
Of human sheep and human kids
To that divine who highest bids.

'Do well in this, and on your head
Unnumbered honours will be shed.'
The agent said, 'Well, truth to tell,
I *have* been doing pretty well.'

'You should,' said Simon, 'at your age;
But now about the parsonage.
How many rooms does it contain?
Show me the photograph again.

'A poor apostle's humble house
Must not be too luxurious;
No stately halls with oaken floor –
It should be decent and no more.

'No billiard-rooms – no stately trees –
No croquet-grounds or pineries.'
'Ah!' sighed the agent, 'very true;
This property won't do for you.

'All these about the house you'll find' –
'Well,' said the parson, 'never mind;
I'll manage to submit to these
Luxurious superfluities.

'A clergyman who does not shirk
The various calls of Christian work,
Will have no leisure to employ
These "common forms" of worldly joy.

'To preach three times on Sabbath days –
To wean the lost from wicked ways –
The sick to soothe – the sane to wed –
The poor to feed with meat and bread;

'These are the various wholesome ways
In which I'll spend my nights and days
My zeal will have no time to cool
At croquet, archery, or pool.'

The agent said, 'From what I hear,
This living will not suit, I fear –
There are no poor, no sick at all;
For services there is no call.'

The reverend gent looked grave. 'Dear me!
Then there is *no* "society"? –
I mean, of course, no sinners there
Whose souls will be my special care?'

The cunning agent shook his head,
'No, none – except ' – (the agent said) –
'The Duke of A., the Earl of B.,
The Marquis C., and Viscount D.

'But you will not be quite alone,
For, though they've chaplains of their own,
Of course this noble well-bred clan
Receive the parish clergyman.'

'Oh, silence, sir!' said Simon M.,
'Dukes – earls! What should I care for them?
These worldly ranks I scorn and flout!'
'Of course,' the agent said, 'no doubt.'

'Yet I might show these men of birth
The hollowness of rank on earth.'
The agent answered, 'Very true –
But I should not, if I were you.'

'Who sells this rich advowson, pray?'
The agent winked – it was his way –
'His name is Hart; 'twixt me and you,
He is, I'm griev'd to say, a Jew!'

'A Jew?' said Simon, 'happy find!
I purchase this advowson, mind.
My life shall be devoted to
Converting that unhappy Jew!'

W. S. GILBERT

Visionary

ON THE ADVANTAGES OF AN 'ASTRAL BODY'

It is told, in Buddhi-theosophic Schools
  There – are rules
By observing which when mundane matter irks
 Or the world has gone amiss, you
 Can incontinently issue
 From the circumscribing tissue
  Of your Works.

That the body and the gentleman inside
    Can divide,
And the latter, if acquainted with the plan,
  Can alleviate the tension
  By remaining 'in suspension'
  As a kind of fourth dimension
    Bogie man.

And to such as mourn an Indian Solar Crime
    At its prime,
'Twere a stratagem so luminously fit,
  That, tho' doctrinaires deny it,
  And Academicians guy it,
  I, for one, would like to try it
    For a bit.

Just to leave one's earthly tenement asleep
    In a heap,
And detachedly to watch it as it lies,
  With an epidermis pickled
  Where the prickly heat has prickled,
  And a sense of being tickled
    By the flies.

And to sit and loaf and idle till the day
    Dies away,
In a duplicate ethereally cool,
  Or around the place to potter,
  (Tho' the flesh could hardly totter,)
  As contented as an otter
    In a pool!

Let the pestilent mosquito do his worst
    Till he burst,
Let him bore and burrow, morning, noon and night,

If he finds the diet sweet, oh,
Who am *I* to place a veto
On the pestilent mosquito?
    Let him bite!

O my cumbersome misfit of bone and skin,
        Could I win
To the wisdom that would render me exempt
    From the grosser bonds that tether
    You and Astral Me together,
    I should simply treat the weather
        With contempt;

I should contemplate its horrors with entire
        Lack of ire,
And pursuant to my comfortable aim,
    With a snap at every shackle
    I should quit my tabernacle,
    And serenely sit and cackle
        At the game!

But, alas! the 'mystic glory swims away',
        And the clay
Is as vulgarly persistent as of yore,
    And the cuticle is pickled
    Where the prickly heat has prickled,
    And the nose and ears are tickled
        As before;

And until the Buddhi-theosophic Schools
        Print the rules
That will bring our tale of sorrows to a close,
    Body mine, though others chide thee,
    And consistently deride thee,
    I shall have to stay inside thee,
        I suppose!

                    J. S. KENDALL (DUM-DUM)

Marron Rechauffé

Proud the Solicitor –
Family Solicitor –
All aboard for Calais and
   The glass set fair,
With Mrs Solicitor
And Miss Solicitor
Snug abaft the paddle-box
   In gay salt air.

Firm the Solicitor
With the Calais Customs:
Letter-to-*The-Times*-and-
   He-Would-Not-Pay;
Mrs Solicitor
Bridled at their poking;
Miss Solicitor
   Looked the other way.

Lordly the Solicitor
At the gilded Crillon:
No-Feather-Beds-and-
   The-Bells-Must-Ring;
Mrs Solicitor
Couldn't bear the Bidet;
Miss Solicitor
   Marvelled at the thing.

Brusque the Solicitor
With the Crillon waiters.
Damning alien messes
   In phrase condign;

Mrs Solicitor
Detected Garlic;
Miss Solicitor
    Partook of Wine.

Grave the Solicitor
Conferring with the Porter
As to entertainment
    That would not cause
Vestal embarrassment
To Miss Solicitor,
Nor would be subversive of
    His Country's laws.

Blithe the Solicitor
Learning from the Porter
All about the Odéon
    And what they played:
Sublimated sentiment,
Flawless Alexandrines,
Totally innocuous
    To man or maid.

Troubled the Solicitor
Rattling to the Odéon –
We-Have-Got-Your-Number-You-
    Must-Drive-With-Care –
By inward stirrings
Not to be mistaken,
Wrathfully ascribable
    To Gallic fare.

Deft the Solicitor,
Desperate-retentive,
Planting loved ones in
    The foremost row;

Quitting them abruptly
To seek mysterious regions
To which Solicitors
    Must sometimes go.

Purged the Solicitor,
Affable-informative
Of Aristotle's Unities
    And much beside;
Dwelling on Purgation
By Horror and Compassion,
And on the ancient tracing
    Of Sin from Pride.

Calm the Solicitor,
Relying on the Porter,
When to ghostly thumpings
    The act-drop rose
On rites most unsuggestive
To Miss Solicitor,
On lantern jaws, on ageing limbs
    In spun-silk hose.

Vexed the Solicitor
To hear above the booming
Of flawless Alexandrines an
    Insistent beat,
A hoarse obbligato,
Pervasive and continuing;
To see a Hag, with claw outheld,
    Beside his seat . . .

Chastened the Solicitor,
Gallic mirth about him,
And Miss Solicitor
    Rosy in dismay:

Monsieur n'a pas payé,
The Beldam chanted,
Monsieur n'a pas payé,
   Son Cabinet.

                                        W. BRIDGES-ADAMS

Polterguest, My Polterguest

I've put Miss Hopper upon the train,
And I hope to do so never again,
For must I do so, I shouldn't wonder
If, instead of upon it, I put her under.

Never has host encountered a visitor
Less desirabler, less exquisiter,
Or experienced such a tangy zest
In beholding the back of a parting guest.

Hoitiful-toitiful Hecate Hopper,
Haunted our house and haunted it proper,
Hecate Hopper left the property
Irredeemably Hecate Hopperty.

The morning paper was her monopoly
She reads it first, and Hecate hopperly,
Handing on to the old subscriber
A wad of Dorothy Dix and fiber.

Shall we coin a phrase for 'to uncooperate'?
How about trying 'to Hecate Hopperate'?
On the maid's days off she found it fun
To breakfast in bed at quarter to one.

Not only was Hecate on a diet,
She insisted that all the family try it,
And all one week-end we gobbled like pigs
On rutabagas and salted figs.

She clogged the pipes and she blew the fuses,
She broke the rocker that Grandma uses,
She left stuff to be posted or expressed,
Hecate Hopper, the Polterguest.

If I pushed Miss Hopper under the train
I'd probably have to do it again,
For the time that I pushed her off the boat
I regretfully found Miss Hopper could float.

OGDEN NASH

Grandmer's Busy Day

BEING A SMALL EXCERPT FROM THE GREAT
AMERICAN LOVE STORY

Grandmer loves granddaughter Beta
But teenage Beta plays with Alpha –
A teenage youth 'clapt Alfred Pie,
We call him Alpha and for why?
For why he were the very first
Would do with Beta that he durst –
And had, but Grandmer hobbling by
Saw them coupling, raised sad cry
'Alack, alas! Alfred! Beta! Stop this inster!
'Two childer about to make a childer!
'Wretched Beta! Art, gal, bust?
'Or didst they Granny hap here fust?'

A frogman with great hands of **mutton**
Who smacks the sea's broad marble bottom
Could not have walloped Beta so!
But Grandmer could, and she knew how!
What time creek frogs intoned the skies
'Better Grandmer's hand than Pie's'.

Over Grandmer's knees bow bent
First red, then white, our Beta went –
A sight to charm young Alfred Pie
That deeming not his personal safety
But inveigled to a closer view
(Panties by Haver Dash & Co.)

He sidled close to Grandmer's arm!
When, gosh! Granny with a ruggled frown
Seized, debagged, and flung him down,
And proceeded in a merry din
Alternately biffing Beta, and biffing him.

The goggling frogs who heard their groans
While holding humans sorry loons
As Grandmer's flailing arm beat time
Sang in creek refrain this rhyme:

'Promise you'll never do it again
'Do it again
'Do it again
'Promise you'll never do it again
'You limbs of Satan, you!'

Since Granny marked their homework copies
Have A and B found greater glories,
And checked their lustful appetites
By douching the afflicted parts?
So keeping Alpha's inches flaccid
And Beta's Mound of Venus placid?

Alas! For our most earnest hopes
It is not thus they learnt the ropes –
I'd like to show them heavenward bent
With priest's robe, nun's robe, Book, and scent,
Or in a chariot lifted up
(Elevators by Neverstop Incorp.)

But not to sell you any pup
I ween it is between those twain
That once is seen: that twice is not seen!
For now when Grandmer nods *they* wink ...
They're up to something, I should think.

EWART MILNE

The Bleed'n' Sparrer

We 'ad a bleed'n' sparrer wot
Lived up a bleed'n' spaht,
One day the bleed'n' rain came dahn
An' washed the bleeder aht.

An' as 'e layed 'arf drahnded
Dahn in the bleed'n' street
'E begged that bleed'n' rainstorm
To bave 'is bleed'n' feet.

But then the bleed'n' sun came aht –
Dried up the bleed'n' rain –
So that bleed'n' little sparrer
'E climbed up 'is spaht again.

But, Oh! – the crewel sparrer'awk,
'E spies 'im in 'is snuggery,
'E sharpens up 'is bleed'n' claws
An' rips 'im aht by thuggery!

Jist then a bleed'n' sportin' type
Wot 'ad a bleed'n' gun
'E spots that bleed'n' sparrer'awk
An' blasts 'is bleed'n' fun.

*

The moral of this story
Is plain to everyone –
That them wot's up the bleed'n' spaht
Don't get no bleed'n' fun.

ANON.

Pirates on Funafuti

Full many a magic island lies within the seas of coral,
But only Funafuti wields a magic that is moral.
There is no island of the East nor in the Spanish Main
That boasts a fauna so correct, a flora so urbane.

It is a pretty sight to see the billows doff their caps
In breaking on the beach, though this is natural perhaps.
The very coconuts that grow so slender in the glades
Incline politely to the winds, though these are only trades.

One sunny day a pirate band approached this happy shore,
Fresh from the looting of a ship, and looking out for more –
Jack Slaughter, Galapago Jim, Sam Stiff and Hairy Hugh,
Cuthbert the Cook and Barmy Bill – they *were* an ugly crew.

The first on Funafuti, as it fell, was Captain Jack,
Whom Sam in swinging round an oar had landed on his back.
And he rose up in the shallows with a murderous grimace –
When an unexpected simper altogether changed his face.

'Your pardon, Mr Stiff,' he said, 'for being in the way.
The fault was mine entirely. Not another word, I pray.'
The crew were dumb. 'Be good enough to join me on the sand.
Come, Mr Galapago Jim. Allow me, Cook, a hand.'

The crew obeyed. They would have feared an angry lion less
Than this perplexing suavity, this painful *politesse*.
But as in turn they disembarked and caught the island's spell
Each felt an impulse to behave unusually well.

Said Jim, 'I happen to have brought a change in my valise.
Do me the honour, sir, I beg, of slipping into these.'
'Your kindly thought,' the Skipper said, 'may well prevent a chill.
Excuse me for a moment.' And he went behind a hill.

And so in all propriety they dined upon the beach,
Restricting their consumption to a single helping each,
And choosing the right cutlery with cultivated ease
For caviare, asparagus, or macaroni cheese.

The evening's pleasure ended with a little tune from Sam.
'You cannot think,' the Captain said, 'how deeply moved I am.
The moonlit scene, the tender words, my mother's favourite song –
I wonder, O my comrades, if a pirate's life is wrong!'

They led him sobbing to his bed, their own tears falling fast;
They tucked him in and held his hand until the fit had passed;
They smoothed his pillow neatly, put his cutlass underneath,
And in a glass beside him popped his artificial teeth.

Then one by one they said their prayers and folded up their clothes,
Forgetful of the ribald jest, the customary oaths;
And with a fairy tale or two they talked themselves asleep
To the murmur of the palm-trees and the gently stirring deep.

They sailed at dawn. And as they left the magic coast behind,
The conduct of the company immediately declined.
Their breakfast was a brutal thing; at lunch they hardly spoke;
By dinner-time civility was treated as a joke.

But still on Funafuti beach the ocean rollers break
With a softly silenced thunder, lest the little turtles wake;
Clams in their crannies hide their yawns; and everything is done
To the perfect satisfaction of the overseeing Sun.

                                                    E. V. RIEU

Initials

I think I hardly ever see
Initials carved on fence or tree
Without recalling little Ted,
(Not lost, but gone, alas, ahead),
Who cut, with insufficient thought,
Initials where he didn't ought.
His mother's eldest sister, Kate,
Had given him, to celebrate
The seventh birthday of his life,
A many-bladed pocket knife,
And this attention to their lad
Made both of Edward's parents glad.
But when his father found, next day,
His pencils sharpened right away,
And ma had swept, on all her fours,
The whittled wood from several floors,
They sternly told their son, 'You can't
Thus use the penknife of your aunt.
Employ it to some purpose, do,
Or we shall have it took from you.'

So Edward sat him, thinking, down,
And after study long and brown
Bethought, 'I might with profit use
My knife to label which is whose
Of all the miscellaneous lot
Of things my family has got.
There's nothing gives me so the pip
As arguments on ownership.'
Now people suffer deep distress
Who find on objects they possess,
On hats and boots, on books and ties,
Initials of enormous size,
Especially if these are made
By penknife with a bluntish blade,
And Edward's people, by his tricks
Were penetrated to their quicks.
His mother darned with might and main
To mend the damage, but in vain;
For patched and stitched she never so,
The lacerations seemed to grow,
While pa, who tried percussive force
Upon the problem at its source,
And doubtless left some pretty prints,
Found Edward was opaque to hints.

Of all the Smiths' possessions far
The proudest was their motor-car.
They kept a special little shed
In which it went at night to bed,
With extra super double bars
To out-manoeuvre burglars.
They kept it bright each day with wax,
And even gladly paid its tax,
While so much had it come to be
A member of the family

They suffered nothing to prevent
It going everywhere they went.
Now Ted had heard, in chance remarks,
Of cars abducted from their parks,
And, thinking that it might increase
The chances of the local police,
With open knife to garage sped
And on that motor's outer tread,
Both back and front and off and near,
Incised initials deep and clear.

Next day his pa and ma and he
Set out for Southport by the sea,
And pa, in packing, came upon
Fresh items with initials on.
This caused delay and, hence, a need
For consequently greater speed.
Small wonder as they seaward tore
Those sculptured outer covers wore
And, mid the traffic at its worst,
ALL SIMULTANEOUSLY BURST!
In vain there rose on every side
The awful screech of brakes applied;
That ordered highway had become
A sort of motor rugger scrum
With, in and underneath it all,
Poor Edward's motor as the ball.

Those gentle readers are correct
Who think no person should expect
From such a tangle to contrive
To extricate himself alive.

H. A. FIELD

A Cautionary Tale

MR THOMAS MEDDLE SENIOR

WHO DID

My tale begins with Junior Tom,
Who made his own Atomic Bomb:
He built it with a clockwork spring,
A photographic flashlight thing,
A detonator found at Chatham,
And a slightly bent Uranium Atom.
Alas! One day, with son at school,
His father, prowling round the tool
Shed in a bored and idle manner,
Straightened the Atom with a spanner!

Six miles away, in the dusty gloom
Of a dismal desk – encumbered room,
The boys abruptly ceased to think
Of Magna Carta, canes, and ink,
But ducked their tuppennies at the flash,
Felt all the building rock and crash,
Then, crawling from beneath the rubble,
Bewildered by the hubble-bubble,
And sitting up in startled crowd,
Beheld a monstrous mushroom cloud,
Fantastically broad and high,
Surge blackly up into the sky ...

Said Junior Tom, 'How like the Pater!
Bang goes my only detonator!'

J. A. LINDON

The Naiad of Ostend

(Based on a passage in T. A. Trollope's *What I remember*
concerning a young lady 'killed by over-bathing')

I. THE ARRIVAL

Ostend, eighteen thirty-five –
   Don't you know the reason
For the crowds along the front?
   It's the bathing season!

Kursaal windows flashing bright,
   Bands and fountains busy,
Pigeon-shooting, valsing, loo –
   Enough to turn you dizzy.

Such a press of elegance,
   Fribbles, belles, and smarties,
Feathered heads and painted fans,
   Balls and picnic parties.

Such a flash of carriage-wheels,
   Seas of light to swim in,
Sparkling water, sparkling wine,
   Sparkling eyes of women.

Nightly, nightly now the moon
   Lights the dreaming ocean,
And at noon towards it flows
   The muslin tide of fashion.

Into this amusing world
   By the dancing-water
Enter Mrs Mackintosh
   And Margaret, her daughter.

Fresh from Paris, full of charm,
    The widow sports a bonnet
Envied for the tartan bows
    And ears of corn upon it.

Margaret is just nineteen,
    Tall as any goddess –
Dian in that springy step,
    Juno in that bodice.

Belgians marvel at her bloom,
    Flâneurs at her figure –
Highland mists for rosy cheeks,
    Breakfast oats for vigour.

'Mother, mother, may I bathe?'
    'Yes, my darling daughter!
See the gaily striped machines
    Drawn up to the water.'

'Mother, mother, may I bathe?'
    '*Again*, my darling daughter?
'Ostend is so very hot,
    It's heaven in the water.'

'Mother, mother, may I bathe?'
    'Meg, my darling daughter,
I can't think where you get it from,
    This passion for the water.'

2. THE COMMENT

'Your daughter seems to adore
    Above all things the sea –
She *shuns* the land, Madame,'
    'Monsieur, you're telling me!'

'Three times a day she bathes,
   She finds Ostend so hot.'
'Madame, a dip is good;
   Excess, I fear, is not.'

'Indeed, I sometimes fear
   Some secret strange allure,
And yet I know the sea
   Is above all things pure;

'The sea's her element,
   She loves to feel aloof.'
'Ah, but a Mackintosh
   Should be more waterproof.'

3. SOCIAL EVENINGS

Fashionables delight in
   Evenings at the Fauches',
Pleasant English visitors
   Attentive on the couches;

Madame B., in yellow silk,
   Fingering the spinet,
Mary Fauche, the Consul's wife,
   Singing like a linnet.

Here and there an *oeillade*,
   A look of *carpe diem* –
'Taste these sweets, they're tempting,
   Just to please me, try 'em!'

Ripe in burning August moon
   Over midnight ocean –
Neptune's manly bosom heaves
   With a deep emotion.

'Mother, mother, may I swim?'
   'What, *at night*, my daughter?
The bathing-women have gone home,
   There's *no one* in the water!'

Now the nights are dry and warm,
   And the moon grows bigger,
All the married couples dance
   The chassée-croisez figure.

Madame L., the banker's wife,
   Writes to Captain Smithett,
Sending him a billet-doux
   And a latchkey with it –

'*Toi qui commandes la Flèche
   Peux commander les cœurs –*'
History will not relate
   How he answers her.

Colonel Dickson likes to give
   Dinner parties often;
When he looks at Margaret
   His martial features soften.

Baron Melfort makes himself
   Sweet as sugar candy,
But she never turns a glance
   On that randy dandy.

Margaret turns her head away,
   Feeling bored and pestered,
Turns her lovely sea-green eyes
   Outward, seaward, westward.

4. THE REPROACH

'Margaret, I wish to find
    A husband for my daughter,
But ever since we came you seem
    Quite wedded to the water.

'The Baron with his quizzing-glass
    And wealthy Colonel Dickson
Must think you not a naiad but
    Some kind of water-vixen;

'Each is looking for a wife,
    But neither man has got a
Wish to join his fortunes with
    A two-legged female otter.

'Come out, my girl, and dry yourself,
    And let me see your figure,
Come out before your skin gets burnt
    As black as any nigger!'

'Mother, mother, I must bathe!
    Your own unruly daughter
Has found the truest, bluest bliss
    Awaits her in the water.'

5. ECSTASY

Neptune loves the breast-stroke
    As Margaret loves the sea,
And now it is his best joke
    To keep her from her tea;

While mother bakes in dudgeon
    Beneath the hot sea-wall,
And sees her do the trudgen,
    And sees her do the crawl,

Neptune smooths each contour,
    Each long elastic leg,
With not a soul *à l'entour*
    Embraces blooming Meg;

As supple as a porpoise
    She welcomes his advances –
Ah, Neptune, *habeas corpus!*
    The gods have all the chances.

6. THE DECLINE

August grows older,
    Thunder in the air,
The pace grows slower
    In this gay Ostend,
And tarnished summer
    Seems to declare
That light abandon
    Meets a heavy end.

Parasols are folded,
    Awnings fade,
Fans still flutter
    In the afternoon shade,
They're eating ices
    In the Royal Arcade,
Soon it will be time for
    Bills to be paid.

'*Madame! et comment*
    Se porte-t-elle
Mees Marguerite?
    D'une taille si belle!'

'Thank you, she's not
   Herself, I'm afraid –
Even upon her
   This heat must tell;

'She has eaten nothing
   Since Saturday night,
And seems so languid –
   It can't be right –
I'm quite alarmed –
   Uncommon pallor –
I do protest she
   Looks quite yaller.'

7. THE END

'Mother, mother, one more bathe!'
   'Is it wise, my daughter?
I vow you owe this lassitude
   To long hours in the water.

'That is what the doctor thinks;
   Now wouldn't it be wiser
To listen to the counsel of
   Your medical adviser?

'You say the sea alone can cool
   This low and wasting fever,
But truly, truly Neptune is
   Like all men, a deceiver.'

Margaret gave her mother then
   A look that might appal,
And with a last low moan she turned
   Her face toward the wall –
   And that was all.

8. THE EPITAPH

Here lies the Naiad of Ostend
   Who swam to an untimely end,
But now with her the Cherubim
   Delight in Seas of Grace to swim;
O happy Mackintosh, to share
   That everlasting *bain de mer!*

WILLIAM PLOMER

Galoshes

I am having a *rapprochement* with galoshes
And some would say this heralds middle age;
Yes, sneering they would say
'Does he also wear pince-nez?
Old jossers wore galoshes when ladies' hats were cloches,
Ha! Woollen combinations are this dodderer's next stage!'
Well, let these people snigger
Just because my feet look bigger,
For, colossal in galoshes, they are dry among the sploshes;
A story that won't wash is this notion that galoshes,
So snug at slushy crossings, make a man a sloppy figure.

Oh, crossly, and still crosslier,
I have bought shoes ever costlier
Which, still quite new, let water through before I've crossed the street:
There's nothing manly, I repeat,
In always having cold wet feet;
Galoshlessness is foolishness when sharply slants the sleet –
And I utterly refuse
The expression 'overshoes',
To make galoshes posher I would scorn this feeble ruse.
The word 'galosh' is strong, not weak,

It comes from *kalopous*, the Greek
For 'cobbler's last', and thus it's classed with hero times antique.
Come, Muse, through slush and sleet dry-footed with me trip so
That I may praise galoshes in a *kalopous* calypso.
    Oh, when swishing buses splash
    And the rush-hour masses clash
When it's marshy as molasses, how galoshes cut a dash!
    It makes me quite impassioned
    When they're dubbed unsmart, old-fashioned –
    (For such, by gosh, the bosh is that's talked about galoshes)
    Since the very finest leather
    Is outsmarted altogether
By the classy, glossy polish of galoshes in such weather.

    Come, galoshers, be assertive,
    Drop that air discreet and furtive!
    Let galosh shops' stocks be lavish
    With designs and hues that ravish –
    Men's galoshes black and British, but for ladies colours skittish
    (And galoshes could make rings
    Round those silly plastic things
    Which tie up with clumsy strings) –
Let us *all* have this *rapprochement* with galoshes
And see what health and happiness it brings!

PAUL JENNINGS

Advice to a Young Lady on the Subject of Alcohol

Beware the man who keeps you late
When Mum said to be in by ate,
And shun the chap who, at the Palais,
Invites you to inspect his chalais.
Behave, then, as you really ought,
Refuse that second glass of pought.
Supping unaccustomed liquor
Will only make you fall the quicor;
Drinking brandies at 'The Mitre'
Is sure to go and make you titre;
And oh! that headache in the dawn
Will make you wish you'd not been bawn.
Remember, then, a maiden oughter
Shun all drink and stick to woughter.

ERIC PARROTT

UNNATURAL HISTORY

The Coelacanth

A DIALOGUE ON EVOLUTION

'*Melania Anjouani*, the Coelacanth, has never evolved.'
– Professor Smith

There lived a happy coelacanth
In dim, primordial seas,
He ate and mated, hunted, slept,
Completely at his ease.
Dame Nature urged: 'Evolve!'
He said: 'Excuse me, Ma'am,
You get on making Darwin,
I'm staying as I am.'

The fishes changed their fishy shapes,
The reptiles stormed the land,
The algae turned to trees, the apes
To men, we understand.
The Coelacanth remained
A monster and a myth;
He said: 'There's nothing to be gained
By my becoming Smith.'

Dame Nature urged: 'You must desire,
And what you wish you'll be it.
Surely, "we needs must love the higher",'
She quoted, ' "when we see it".'
The Coelacanth said: 'Hark!
It all depends on what
You mean by "higher": Me, Lamarck,
Or Alfred, does it no

'To be a whirlpool of Pure Mind
That surely is the goal,'
She begged, 'Until you are, you find,
No body, but all soul.'
The Coelacanth just set
His square, determined jaw.
'Then leave me out,' he snapped, 'and get
On with Bernard Shaw.'

So for a hundred million years
While Nature worked out man the
Obdurate Coelacanth appears
The same, and simply perseveres
In being Coelacanthi.

HORACE SHIPP

The Fall

The Garden of Eden (described in the Bible)
Was Guinness's Brewery (mentioned by Joyce),
Where innocent Adam and Eve were created
And dwelt from necessity rather than choice;

For nothing existed but Guinness's Brewery,
Guinness's Brewery occupied all,
Guinness's Brewery everywhere, anywhere –
Woe that expulsion succeeded the Fall!

The ignorant pair were encouraged in drinking
Whatever they fancied whenever they could –
Except for the porter or stout which embodied
Delectable knowledge of Evil and Good.

In Guinness's Brewery, innocent, happy,
They tended the silos and coppers and vats,
They polished the engines and coppered the barrels
And even made pets of the brewery rats.

One morning while Adam was brooding and brewing
It happened that Eve had gone off on her own
When a serpent like ivy slid up to her softly
And murmured seductively, Are we alone?

'O Eve,' said the serpent, 'I beg you to sample
A bottle of Guinness's excellent stout,
Whose nutritive qualities no one can question
And stimulant properties no one can doubt;

'It's tonic, enlivening, strengthening, heartening,
Loaded with vitamins, straight from the wood,
And further enriched with the not undesirable
Lucrative knowledge of Evil and Good.'

So Eve was persuaded and Adam was tempted;
They fell and they drank and continued to drink,
(Their singing and dancing and shouting and prancing
Prevented the serpent from sleeping a wink).

Alas, when the couple had finished a barrel
And swallowed the final informative drops,
They looked at each other and knew they were naked
And covered their intimate bodies with hops.

The anger and rage of the Lord were appalling,
He wrathfully cursed them for taking to drink
And hounded them out of the brewery, followed
By beetles (magenta) and elephants (pink).

The crapulous couple emerged to discover
A universe full of diseases and crimes
Where porter could only be purchased for money
In specified places at specified times.

And now in this world of confusion and error
Our only salvation and hope is to try
To threaten and bargain our way into Heaven
By drinking the heavenly brewery dry.

FERGUS ALLEN

Noah

After all the flood-storm's dark
A southern sun shone on the ark.

From the foreland of Hawaii
Floated voices soft and sighy,

From the beaches called: 'Aloha,'
Sweetly called: 'Aloha, Noah,

'Come and be forever harbored.'
Other voices came from starboard,

Called: 'This isle is Noa-Noa;
Welcome, Noah, and aloha;

'Live with us and furl your sail.'
Noah went up to the rail,

(Shouting to an upraised boa:
'Down! you naughty so-and-soa!')

Said: 'How keep my charges waiting?
Spite of orders, they've been mating.

'I've been doing some detecting;
All the ladies are expecting;

'And we've not an inch of space.
This crowded cruise is now a race.

'I must get my charges home,
Have no time for even Rome;

'And you're all so loving here.'
Noah turned to hide a tear;

Said: 'The answer must be noa.
I am Noah; I must goa.'

So he left the siren seas,
Left the luring melodies,

Left the loving maidens flat;
Ran aground on Ararat.

O those islands! O those seas!
O those siren melodies!

Hark! I hear that sweet Aloha.
Am I yes or am I Noah?

CLARK STILLMAN

The Apple-Dumplings and a King

Once on a time, a Monarch, tired with whooping,
    Whipping, and spurring,
    Happy in worrying
A poor, defenceless, harmless Buck
(The horse and rider wet as muck),
From his high consequence and wisdom stooping,
    Entered, through curiosity, a cot
Where sat a poor Old Woman and her pot.

The wrinkled, blear-eyed, good old Granny,
In this same cot, illumed by many a cranny,
    Had finished Apple-dumplings for her pot.
In tempting row the naked Dumplings lay,
When, lo! the Monarch, in his *usual* way,
    Like Lightning spoke: 'What's this? what's this?
        what? what?'

Then, taking up a Dumpling in his hand,
His eyes with admiration did expand,
    And oft did Majesty the Dumpling grapple:
''Tis monstrous, monstrous hard indeed', he cried:
'What makes it, pray, so hard?' – The Dame replied,
    Low curtseying, 'Please your Majesty, the Apple.' –

'Very astonishing indeed! strange thing!'
(Turning the Dumpling round, rejoined the King).
    ''Tis most extraordinary then, all this is;
    It beats Pinetti's conjuring all to pieces:
Strange I should never of a Dumpling dream!
But, Goody, tell me where, where, where's the Seam?' –

'Sir, there's no seam', quoth she; 'I never knew
That folks did Apple-dumplings *sew*.' –
'No!' cried the staring Monarch with a grin:
'How, how the devil got the Apple in?'

On which the Dame the curious scheme revealed
By which the Apple lay so sly concealed;
   Which made the Solomon of Britain start:
Who to the Palace with full speed repaired,
And Queen and Princesses so beauteous scared,
   All with the wonders of the Dumpling Art.

There did he labour one whole week, to show
   The wisdom of an Apple-dumpling Maker;
And, lo! so deep was Majesty in dough,
   The Palace seemed the lodging of a Baker.

JOHN WOLCOT (PETER PINDAR)

The Man in the Moon

Said the Raggedy Man, on a hot afternoon:
  My!
    Sakes!
      What a lot o' mistakes
Some little folks make on The Man in The Moon!
But people that's be'n up to *see* him, like me,
And calls on him frequent and intimuttly,
Might drop a few facts that would interest you
  Clean!
    Through! –
      If you wanted 'em to –
Some *actual* facts that might interest you!

O The Man in The Moon has a crick in his back;
  Whee!
    Whimm!
      Ain't you sorry for him?
And a mole on his nose that is purple and black;
And his eyes are so weak that they water and run
If he dares to *dream* even he looks at the sun, –
So he jes dreams of stars, as the doctors advise –
  My!
    Eyes!
      But isn't he wise –
To jes dream of stars, as the doctors advise?

And The Man in the Moon has a boil on his ear –
  Whee!
    Whing!
      What a singular thing!
I know! but these facts are authentic, my dear, –
There's a boil on his ear; and a corn on his chin –
He calls it a dimple – but dimples stick in –
Yet it might be a dimple turned over, you know!
  Whang!
    Ho!
      Why, certainly so!
It might be a dimple turned over, you know!

And The Man in the Moon has a rheumatic knee –
  Gee!
    Whizz!
      What a pity that is!
And his toes have worked round where his heels ought
    to be. –
So whenever he wants to go North he goes *South*,
And comes back with porridge-crumbs all round his mouth
And he brushes them off with a Japanese fan,

Whing!
  Whann!
    What a marvellous man!
What a very remarkably marvellous man!

And The Man in the Moon, sighed The Raggedy Man,
  Gits!
    So!
      Sullonsome, you know!, –
Up there by hisse'f sence creation began! –
That when I call on him and then come away,
He grabs me and holds me and begs me to stay, –
Till – *Well!* if it wasn't fer *Jimmy-cum-jim,*
  Dadd!
    Limb!
      I'd go pardners with him –
Jes jump my job here and be pardners with *him!*

J. W. RILEY

Hall and Knight

OR

$$z + b + x = y + b + z$$

When he was young his cousins used to say of Mr Knight:
'This boy will write an Algebra – or looks as if he might.'
And sure enough when Mr Knight had grown to be a man,
He purchased pen and paper and an inkpot, and began.

But he very soon discovered that he couldn't write at all,
And his heart was filled with yearnings for a certain Mr Hall;
Till, after thirty years of doubt, he sent his friend a card:
'Have tried to write an Algebra, but find it very hard.'

Now Mr Hall himself had tried to write a book for schools,
But suffered from a handicap: he didn't know the rules.
So when he heard from Mr Knight and understood his gist,
He answered him by telegram: 'Delighted to assist.'

So Mr Hall and Mr Knight they took a house together,
And they worked away at algebra in any kind of weather,
Determined not to give it up until they had evolved
A problem so constructed that it never could be solved.

'How hard it is,' said Mr Knight, 'to hide the fact from youth
That x and y are equal: it is such an obvious truth!'
'It is,' said Mr Hall, 'but if we gave a b to each,
We'd put the problem well beyond our little victims' reach.

'Or are you anxious, Mr Knight, lest any boy should see
The utter superfluity of this repeated b?'
'I scarcely fear it,' he replied, and scratched his grizzled head,
'But perhaps it *would* be safer if to b we added z.'

'A brilliant stroke!' said Hall, and added z to either side;
Then looked at his accomplice with a flush of happy pride.
And Knight, he winked at Hall (a very pardonable lapse).
And they printed off the Algebra and sold it to the chaps.

E. V. RIEU

Undiscovered History

Catherine of Aragon
Stole a quart jar of Tarragon.
'It's the last in the bin,'
She informed Anne Boleyn.
'It's lovely, give me more!'
Entreated Jane Seymour,
Which made Anne of Cleves
Spill a lot down her sleeves.
'Not for me; I'm a coward!'
Said Catherine Howard.
But Catherine Parr
Drank the rest of the jar.

BRIAN HILL

Life of a Scientist

Isaac Newton, it is reckoned,
Lived in the time of Charles the Second.
Charles's forte was depravity
But Isaac came out strong for gravity.

I. KENVYN EVANS

Pepys' Diary

The Shorter Pepys I've edited:
'Up betimes, and so to bed.'

CLARK STILLMAN

Hengist and Horsa

Hengist was coarser than Horsa,
And Horsa was awfully coarse.
Horsa drank whiskey,
Told tales that were risqué,
But Hengist was in a divorce.
Horsa grew coarser and coarser,
But Hengist was coarse all his life.
That reprobate Horsa
Drank tea from a saucer,
But Hengist ate peas with his knife.

DESMOND CARTER

Casanova

(buried somewhere in the cemetery at Dux in Bohemia)

No one could find his grave for relic-plunder,
    But legend said it would have paid to search
The one whose cross *would* get entangled under
    The skirts of young girls on their way to Church.

RICHARD USBORNE

Note for the Scientist

People who have three daughters try once more
And then it's fifty-fifty they'll have four.
Those with a son or sons will let things be.
Hence all these surplus women. Q.E.D.

JUSTIN RICHARDSON

The Snail

Where is the poet fired to sing
    The snail's discreet degrees,
A rhapsody of sauntering,
    A gloria of ease,
Proclaiming theirs the baser part
    Who consciously forswear
The delicate and gentle art
    Of never getting there.

E. V. LUCAS

Low Love Life

The female spider
Can't abider
Husband
Till he's tucked
Insider.

IVOR C. F. TREBY

A centipede was happy quite,
    Until a frog in fun
Said, 'Pray, which leg comes after which?'
This raised her mind to such a pitch,
She lay distracted in a ditch
    Considering how to run.

MRS EDMUND CRASTER

Anxious Lines on a New Kitten

Is this small ball of fur a noedipus,
Or just a budding feline Oedipus?
Will he, with lavish milk by me supplied,
Quickly forget his new-left mother's side?
Or, complex-fixed, become a – groedipus?

PENDENNIS CASTLE

The Porcupine

Any hound a porcupine nudges
Can't be blamed for harbouring grudges.
I know one hound that laughed all winter
At a porcupine that sat on a splinter.

OGDEN NASH

The Octopus

Tell me, O Octopus, I begs,
Is those things arms, or is they legs?
I marvel at thee, Octopus;
If I were thou, I'd call me Us.

OGDEN NASH

The Sea-Gull

Hark to the whimper of the sea-gull;
He weeps because he's not an ea-gull.
Suppose you were, you silly sea-gull,
Could you explain it to your she-gull?

OGDEN NASH

The Ant

The ant has made himself illustrious
Through constant industry industrious.
So what?
Would you be calm and placid
If you were full of formic acid?

OGDEN NASH

The Jellyfish

Who wants my jellyfish?
I'm not sellyfish!

OGDEN NASH

The Fly

The Lord in His wisdom made the fly,
And then forgot to tell us why.

OGDEN NASH

The Dog

The truth I do not stretch or shove
When I state the dog is full of love.
I've also found, by actual test,
A wet dog is the lovingest.

OGDEN NASH

The Frog

What a wonderful bird the frog are!
When he stand he sit almost;
When he hop he fly almost.
He ain't got no sense hardly;
He ain't got no tail hardly either.
When he sit, he sit on what he ain't got almost.

ANON.

The Elephant

OR

The Force of Habit

A tail behind, a trunk in front,
Complete the usual elephant.
The tail in front, the trunk behind,
Is what you very seldom find.
If you for specimens should hunt
With trunks behind and tails in front,
That hunt would occupy you long;
The force of habit is so strong.

A. E. HOUSMAN

The Squid

The squid has an id;
Id is not nice, but the squid loves id.

CLARK STILLMAN

The Dshy

The Dshy's a beast of midnight gloom,
which fills one hour and one room,
and all the time it is aware,
that maybe it may not be there.

Beware the Dshy, my child, beware
the Dshy, that is not anywhere,
because the beasts we all do know,
are rarely really ever so.

Beware the beasts we cannot see,
they lack responsibility.
The Dshy's not true, and knows it too,
that's why it likes to frighten you.

My child, be careful and don't dare
a Dshy, it may not know you're there.
Nor can you tell when it has gone
because you don't know if there's one.

Beware the beasts which don't exist,
they grab you nightly by the wrist.
Those horrors, like the awful Dshy
which can not live and can not die.

Don't think about the Dshy at all
lest it or worse may you befall.
Remember, that the Dshy is not,
and that the beast be best forgot.

HANS HESS

The Oocuck

'The cuckoo!' cried my child, the while I slept;
    'Sweet pop, the cuckoo! o, its cries impinge!
The harbinger is here!' And up I leapt
    To hear the thing harbinge.

I flung the casement, thrust the visage through,
    Composed the features in rhapsodic look,
Cupped the left ear and ... lo! I heard an 'oo',
    Soon followed by a 'cuck'.

Another 'oo'! A 'cuck'! An 'oo' again.
    A 'cuck'. 'Oocuck'. 'Oocuck' Ditto. Repeat.
I tried to pick the step up but in vain –
    I'd ... 'oo' ... missed ... 'Cuck' ... the beat.

I'd missed the beat. And this would last till June
    And nothing could be done now to catch up –
This fowl would go on hiccuping its tune,
    Hic after beastly cup.

'Oocuck!' ... 'Oocuck!' ... that was four weeks ago,
    Four non-stop weeks of contrapuntal blight.
My nerves are ... what was that? ... Ah, no! Ah, no!
    Spare me the ingalenight!

JUSTIN RICHARDSON

The Daddy Long-Legs and the Fly

Once Mr Daddy Long-Legs,
   Dressed in brown and gray,
Walked about upon the sands
   Upon a summer's day;
And there among the pebbles,
   When the wind was rather cold,
He met with Mr Floppy Fly,
   All dressed in blue and gold.
And as it was too soon to dine,
They drank some Periwinkle-wine,
And played an hour or two, or more,
At battlecock and shuttledore.

Said Mr Daddy Long-Legs
   To Mr Floppy Fly,
'Why do you never come to court?
   'I wish you'd tell me why.
'All gold and shine, in dress so fine,
   'You'd quite delight the court.
'Why do you never go at all?
   'I really think you *ought!*
'And if you went, you'd see such sights!
'Such rugs! and jugs! and candle-lights!
'And more than all, the King and Queen,
'One in red, and one in green!'

'O Mr Daddy Long-Legs,'
Said Mr Floppy Fly,
'It's true I never go to court,
   'And I will tell you why.
'If I had six long legs like yours,
   'At once I'd go to court!

'But Oh! I can't, because *my* legs
    'Are so extremely short.
'And I'm afraid the King and Queen
'(One in red and one in green)
'Would say aloud, "You are not fit,
' "You Fly, to come to court a bit!"

'O Mr Daddy Long-Legs,'
    Said Mr Floppy Fly,
'I wish you'd sing one little song!
    'One mumbian melody!
'You used to sing so awful well
    'In former days gone by,
'But now you never sing at all;
    'I wish you'd tell me why:
'For if you would, the silvery sound
'Would please the shrimps and cockles round,
'And all the crabs would gladly come
'To hear you sing, "Ah, Hum di Hum!" '

Said Mr Daddy Long-Legs,
    'I can never sing again!
'And if you wish, I'll tell you why,
    'Although it gives me pain.
'For years I could not hum a bit,
    'Or sing the smallest song;
'And this the dreadful reason is,
    'My legs are grown too long!
'My six long legs, all here and there,
'Oppress my bosom with despair;
'And if I stand, or lie, or sit,
'I cannot sing one single bit!'

So Mr Daddy Long-Legs
    And Mr Floppy Fly

Sat down in silence by the sea,
   And gazed upon the sky.
They said, 'This is a dreadful thing!
   'The world has all gone wrong,
'Since one has legs too short by half,
   'The other much too long!
'One never more can go to court,
'Because his legs have grown too short;
'The other cannot sing a song,
'Because his legs have grown too long!'

Then Mr Daddy Long-Legs
   And Mr Floppy Fly
Rushed downward to the foaming sea
   With one sponge-taneous cry;
And there they found a little boat
   Whose sails were pink and gray;
And off they sailed among the waves
   Far, and far away.
They sailed across the silent main
And reached the great Gromboolian plain;
And there they play for evermore
At battlecock and shuttledore.

EDWARD LEAR

Professor Todlipp's Love-Child

Many an eminent Man of Science
Has made a dismal misalliance
And met Displeasure with Defiance.
Many a famous Man of Learning
Has taken wildly the Wrong Turning
And never Known his Ears were burning.

But Professor Todlipp's Fall from Grace –
A squalid biologic case –
Profoundly shocked the Human Race;
For Frog–Man Cross Insemination
Must move to sombre cogitation
Even readers of 'N.S. and Nation'.

Professor Todlipp had no Wife
In all the Ups and Downs of Life,
Avoided Matrimonial Strife
By living with an Only Sister
In a villa 'Bella Vista'
Sexless as the Aspidistra.

Professor Todlipp did not mind
The plain, flat face of Female Kind,
But he found it less refined –
Of whatsoever race or nation,
Latin, Nordic, Negroid, Asian –
Than the goggle-eyed Batrachian.

The Professor's softest cardiac spot
Lay not with Blonde or Hottentot,
But with frogs – amphibious lot:
Frogs that hopped and frogs that climbed,
Frogs that croaked and frogs that chimed,
Frogs unclassified, unrhymed.

There came by Air Mail one bluff day
From the green steams of Paraguay
Unfertilized frogspawn in a tray.
Professor Todlipp deaf (and dumb)
To any sense of what might come
Took a needle, pricked his thumb.

With that needle, now lymphatic,
Advanced upon the tray, ecstatic,
Pricked the spawn in gesture Attic
Then turning to his Only Sister
Remarked as soberly he kissed her
'Observe, my dear, that little Blister.'

That little blister quickly grew
A head, a tail, and features too
'Now here's a Merry How d'ye do,'
remarked Miss Todlipp, limp with shame
(And that Blister soon became
A Blot upon the Family Name!).

A tadpole first it swam apace
But oh! Sad Omen of Disgrace
Above the tail poor Todlipp's face!
And when the frogling left its jar
And hopped across the Axminster
It hailed them each as 'Ma' and 'Pa'.

Fingers fluttering to her fichu
Pink Miss Todlipp cried 'That creature!
Oh Percival, that froggy's You!
Look at its Eyes! Behold its Nose!
The way it swivels on its toes!
This must be kept Beneath the Rose.'

Professor Todlipp only smiled
'This is not mine, but Science' Child,
When Huckster sees it, he'll be wild ...'
But wilder far, Miss Todlipp wailed
That people had for Less been Jailed ...
So Decorous Secrecy prevailed.

Adopted then by Legal Writ
Young Todlipp grew in Strength and Wit
Though as to Beauty – not a bit,
And to explain the Family Looks
Miss Todlipp still on Tenterhooks
Invents a scapegrace Cousin 'Brooks'.

As the Todlipp's Adopted Son
Brooks Todlipp is embarked upon
His School career at Dartington
Where psychiatrist Tutors, night and day,
Watch the Young Intellect at Play
And guide it gently on its Way.

Among young intellectual creatures,
Surrounded by far sighted Teachers
Young Brooks might well live down his Features.
But in the Underwater Race
By winning at a Startling pace
He earned the nickname 'Froggyface'.

No blemish in his school Career
Could cause his Foster Parents fear,
Unless the Fact they came to hear
That Brooks would turn to palest Ochre
Muttering obscenely as a Stoker
At any glimpse of Tapioca.

Alas, at Oxford (Balliol College)
Brooks attained to sourer Knowledge
And set his Tutors' teeth on edge
And put all Balliol in Amaze
By hopping up the Broad in Stays,
Reciting Kinsey, verse and phrase.

A step from here in the Woodstock Road
A female student, Madge, abode
Squat and Repulsive as a Toad.
And Cupid let his Arrows fly
As one chill morning in July
Brooks Todlipp saw her cycling by.

If Madge and her fiancé Brooks
Were matched in Lung as matched in Looks
Or had read old Todlipp's books
Instead of Kinsey's, then their Fate
Might be the Normal Married State.
But *Frogs need Water when they Mate.*

In Cherwell Pools the mud is deep
And speckled trout cavort and leap
Above them in their Amorous Sleep:
A lasting sleep for One at least.
For Madge there'll be no Wedding Feast,
Bubbles her swansong, *Chanson triste.*

*

The Professor takes the Witness stand
'Am I supposed to Understand ...?'
And Counsel leaves him quite unmanned.
Miss Todlipp, fainting in her Chair
Is brought round whinnying like a Mare
By one Prolonged Judicial Stare.

Miss Todlipp's lips at last unsealed
The Professor's Secret is Revealed
(In Crime Reporter's code: 'She squealed.')
And all those Well-dressed Women too
Who'd spent the Whole Night in a queue
Made a most Horrible to-do,

Until his Lordship in a Fury
Declares Old Bailey's not Old Drury
And threatens to eject the Jury.
Then as the Jurymen retire
The Press Men corner every Wire
To give the World the Tale Entire.

'Guilty, my Lord – but he's half Frog'
The usual Juridicial fog
Had lifted to reveal this Bog.
But the Judge with Shaking Wig
Declares One Witness was a Pig,
Unnamed, Professor Thingamajig:

Wishes the Law allowed the Cat
For retrospective Morals that
Would scarify the Common Rat:
Then Black Cap, Sheeps Wool, Scarlet Gown,
With solemn Words and Ogrish Frown
Orders Brooks Todlipp be Put Down.

The Moral of the Tale of course
Should be Flashed round the World in Morse
'Don't Wolf your Tart before the Sauce'.

SHAMUS FRAZER

THE SADNESS OF THINGS

Song

TO THE TUNE OF 'PADDY'S WEDDING

Queen Dido at
Her palace gate
Sat darning of her stocking O;
She sung and drew
The worsted through,
Whilst her foot was the cradle rocking O;
(For a babe she had
By a soldier lad,
Though hist'ry passes it over O);
'You tell-tale brat,
I've been a flat,
Your daddy has proved a rover O.
What a fool was I
To be cozen'd by
A fellow without a penny O;
When rich ones came,
And ask'd the same,
For I'd offers from never so many O;
But I'll darn my hose,
Look out for beaux,
And quickly get a new lover O;
Then come, lads, come,
Love beats the drum,
And a fig for Aeneas the rover O.'

W. B. RHODES

In Isas Bed

I love in Isas bed to lie
O such a joy and luxury
The bottom of the bed I sleep
And with great care I myself keep
Oft I embrace her feet of lillys
But she has goton all the pillies
Her neck I never can embrace
But I do hug her feet in place
But I am sure I am contented
And of my follies am repented

I am sure I'd rather be
In a small bed at liberty

MARJORY FLEMING

Shadows

Deep! I own I start at shadows,
    Listen, I will tell you why
(Life itself is but a taper,
    Casting shadows till we die).

Once, in Italy, at Florence,
    I a radiant girl adored:
When she came, she saw, she conquered,
    And by Cupid I was floored.

Round my heart her glossy ringlets
    Were mysteriously entwined –
And her soft voluptuous glances
    All my inner thoughts divined.

'Mia cara Mandolina!
　Are we not, indeed,' I cried,
'All the world to one another?'
　Mandolina smiled and sighed.

Earth was Eden, she an angel,
　I, a Jupiter enshrined –
Till one night I saw a damning
　Double shadow on her blind!

'Fire and fury! double shadows
　On their bedroom windows ne'er,
To my knowledge have been cast by
　Ladies virtuous and fair.

'False, abandoned Mandolina!
　Fare thee well, for evermore!
Vengeance!' shrieked I, 'vengeance, vengeance!'
　And I thundered through the door.

This event occurred next morning;
　Mandolina staring sat,
Stark amazed, as out I tumbled,
　Raving mad, without a hat!

Six weeks after I'd a letter,
　On its road six weeks delayed –
With a dozen re-directions
　From the lost one, and it said:

'Foolish, wicked, cruel Albert!
　Base suspicion's doubts resign;
Double lights throw double shadows!
　Mandolina – ever thine!'

'Heavens, what an ass!' I muttered,
     'Not before to think of that!' –
And again I rushed excited
     To the rail, without a hat.

'Mandolina! Mandolina!'
     When her house I reached, I cried:
'Pardon, dearest love!' she answered –
     'I'm the Russian Consul's bride!'

Thus, by Muscovite barbarian,
     And by Fate, my life was crossed;
Wonder ye I start at shadows?
     Types of Mandolina lost.

ANON.

The Ballad of the Green Old Man

It was a balmeous day in May, when spring was springing high
And all among the buttercups the bees did butterfly;
While the butterflies were being enraptured in the flowers,
And winsome frogs were singing soft morals to the showers.

Green were the emerald grasses which grew upon the plain,
And green too were the verdant boughs which rippled in the rain,
Far green likewise the apple hue which clad the distant hill,
And at the station sat a man who looked far greener still.

An ancient man, a boy-like man, a person mild and meek,
A being who had little tongue, and nary bit of cheek.
And while upon him pleasant-like I saw the ladies look,
He sat a-counting money in a brownsome pocket-book.

Then to him a policeman spoke: 'Unless you feel too proud,
You'd better stow away that cash while you're in this here crowd;
There's many a chap about this spot who'd clean you out like ten.'
'And can it be', exclaimed the man, 'there are such wicked men?'

'Then I will put my greenbacks up all in my pocket-book,
And keep it buttoned very tight, and at the button look.'
He said it with a simple tone, and gave a simple smile –
You never saw a half-grown shad one-half so void of guile.

And the bumble-bees kept bumbling away among the flowers,
While distant frogs were frogging amid the summer showers,
And the tree-toads were tree-toadying in accents sharp or flat –
All nature seemed a-naturing as there the old man sat.

Then up and down the platform promiscuous he strayed,
Amid the waiting passengers he took his lemonade,
A-making little kind remarks unto them all at sight,
Until he met two travellers who looked cosmopolite.

Now even as the old was green, this pair were darkly-brown;
They seemed to be of that degree that sports about the town
Amid terrestrial mice, I ween, their destiny was Cat;
If ever men were gonoffs,* I should say these two were that.

And they had watched that old man well with interested look,
And gazed him counting greenbacks in that brownsome pocket-
          book;
And the elder softly warbled with benevolential phiz,
'Green peas has come to market, and the veg'tables is riz.'

Yet still across the heavenly sky the clouds went clouding on.
The rush upon the gliding brook kept rushing all alone,
While the ducks upon the water were a-ducking just the same,
And every mortal human man kept on his little game.

          Yiddish for crooks.

And the old man to the strangers very affable let slip
How that zealousy policeman had given him the tip,
And how his cash was buttoned in his pocket dark and dim,
And how he guessed no man alive on earth could gammon him.

In ardent conversation ere long the three were steeped,
And in that good man's confidence the younger party deeped.
The p'liceman, as he shadowed them, exclaimed in blooming rage,
'They're stuffin' of that duck, I guess, and leavin' out the sage'.

He saw the game distinctly, and inspected how it took,
And watched the reappearance of that brownsome pocket-book,
And how that futile ancient, ere he buttoned up his coat,
Had interchanged, obliging-like, a greensome coloured note,

And how they parted tenderly, and how the happy twain
Went out into the Infinite by taking of the train:
Then up the blue policeman came, and said, 'My ancient son,
Now you have gone and did it; say what you have been and done?'

And unto him the good old man replied in childish glee,
'They were as nice a two young men as I did ever see;
But they were in such misery their story made me cry;
So I lent 'em twenty dollars – which they'll pay me bye-and-bye.

'But as I had no twenty, we also did arrange,
They got from me a fifty bill, and gimme thirty change;
But they will send that fifty back, and by to-morrow's train –'
'That note,' out cried the constable, 'you'll never see again.'

'And that', exclaimed the sweet old man, 'I hope I never may,
Because I do not care a cuss how far it keeps away;
For if I'm a judge of money, and I *reether* think I am,
The one I shoved was never worth a continental dam.

'They hev wandered with their sorrers into the sunny South,
They hev got uncommon swallows and an extry lot of mouth.
In the next train to the North'ard I expect to widely roam,
And if any come inquirin', jist say I ain't at home.'

The p'liceman lifted up his glance unto the sunny skies,
I s'pose the light was fervent, for a tear were in his eyes,
And said, 'If in your travels a hat store you should see,
Just buy yourself a beaver tile and charge that tile to me.'

While the robins were a robbing acrost the meadow gay,
And the pigeons still a-pigeoning among the gleam of May,
All out of doors kept out of doors as suchlike only can,
A-singing of an endless hymn about that good old man.

C. G. LELAND

The Duel

A SERIOUS BALLAD

'Like the two Kings of Brentford smelling at one nosegay.'

In Brentford town, of old renown,
   There lived a Mister Bray,
Who fell in love with Lucy Bell,
   And so did Mr Clay.

To see her ride from Hammersmith,
   By all it was allow'd,
Such fair outsides are seldom seen,
   Such Angels on a Cloud.

Said Mr Bray to Mr Clay,
   You choose to rival me,
And court Miss Bell, but there your court
   No thoroughfare shall be.

Unless you now give up your suit,
    You may repent your love;
I who have shot a pigeon match,
    Can shoot a turtle dove.

So pray before you woo her more,
    Consider what you do;
If you pop aught to Lucy Bell, –
    I'll pop it into you.

Said Mr Clay to Mr Bray,
    Your threats I quite explode;
One who has been a volunteer
    Knows how to prime and load.

And so I say to you unless
    Your passion quiet keeps,
I who have shot and hit bulls' eyes,
    May chance to hit a sheep's.

Now gold is oft for silver changed,
    And that for copper red;
But these two went away to give
    Each other change for lead.

But first they sought a friend a-piece,
    This pleasant thought to give –
When they were dead, they thus should have
    Two seconds still to live.

To measure out the ground not long
    The seconds then forebore,
And having taken one rash step,
    They took a dozen more.

They next prepared each pistol-pan
   Against the deadly strife,
By putting in the prime of death
   Against the prime of life.

Now all was ready for the foes,
   But when they took their stands,
Fear made them tremble so they found
   They both were shaking hands.

Said Mr C. to Mr B.,
   Here one of us may fall,
And like St Paul's Cathedral now,
   Be doom'd to have a ball.

I do confess I did attach
   Misconduct to your name;
If I withdraw the charge, will then
   Your ramrod do the same?

Said Mr B., I do agree –
   But think of Honour's Courts!
If we go off without a shot,
   There will be strange reports.

But look, the morning now is bright,
   Though cloudy it begun;
Why can't we aim above, as if
   We had call'd out the sun?

So up into the harmless air
   Their bullets they did send;
And may all other duels have
   That upshot in the end!

THOMAS HOOD

Dahn the Plug-'ole

A muvver was barfin' 'er biby one night,
The youngest of ten and a tiny young mite,
The muvver was pore and the biby was thin,
Only a skelington covered in skin;
The muvver turned rahnd for the soap orf the rack,
She was but a moment, but when she turned back,
The biby was gorn; and in anguish she cried,
'Oh, where is my biby?' – The angels replied:
'Your biby 'as fell dahn the plug-'ole,
Your biby 'as gorn dahn the plug;
The poor little thing was so skinny and thin
'E oughter been barfed in a jug;
Your biby is perfeckly 'appy,
'E won't need a barf any more,
Your biby 'as fell dahn the plug-'ole,
Not lorst, but gorn before.'

ANON.

My Life is a –

At Worthing an exile from Geraldine G—,
How aimless, how wretched an exile is he!
Promenades are not even prunella and leather
To lovers, if lovers can't foot them together.

He flies the parade, sad by ocean he stands,
He traces a 'Geraldine G—' on the sands,
Only 'G' though her loved patronymic is 'Green' –
I will not betray thee, my own Geraldine.

The fortunes of men have a time and a tide,
And Fate, the old fury, will not be denied;
That name was, of course, soon wiped out by the sea,
– She jilted the exile, did Geraldine G.

They meet, but they never have spoken since that, –
He hopes she is happy – he knows she is fat;
She wooed on the shore, now is wed in the Strand, –
And *I* – it was I wrote her name on the sand!

FREDERICK LOCKER-LAMPSON

The Biter Bit

The sun is in the sky, mother, the flowers are springing fair,
And the melody of woodland birds is stirring in the air;
The river, smiling to the sky, glides onward to the sea,
And happiness is everywhere, oh mother, but with me!

They are going to the church, mother, – I hear the marriage bell;
It booms along the upland, – oh! it haunts me like a knell;
He leads her on his arm, mother, he cheers her faltering step,
And closely to his side she clings, – she does, the demirep!

They are crossing by the stile, mother, where we so oft have stood,
The stile beside the shady thorn, at the corner of the wood;
And the boughs, that wont to murmur back the words that won my
    ear,
Wave their silver blossoms o'er him, as he leads his bridal fere.

He will pass beside the stream, mother, where first my hand he
    pressed,
By the meadow where, with quivering lip, his passion he confessed;
And down the hedgerows where we've strayed again and yet again;
But he will not think of me, mother, his broken-hearted Jane!

He said that I was proud, mother, – that I looked for rank and gold;
He said I did not love him, – he said my words were cold;
He said I kept him off and on, in hopes of higher game, –
And it may be that I did, mother; but who hasn't done the same?

I did not know my heart, mother, – I know it now too late;
I thought that I without a pang could wed some nobler mate;
But no nobler suitor sought me, – and he has taken wing,
And my heart is gone, and I am left a lone and blighted thing.

You may lay me in my bed, mother, – my head is throbbing sore;
And, mother, prithee let the sheets be duly aired before;
And, if you'd do a kindness to your poor desponding child,
Draw me a pot of beer, mother – and, mother, draw it mild!

THEODORE MARTIN

Lost Mr Blake

Mr Blake was a regular out-and-out hardened sinner,
    Who was quite out of the pale of Christianity, so to speak:
He was in the habit of smoking a long pipe and drinking a glass of
        grog on Sunday after dinner,
    And seldom thought of going to church more than twice (or if
        Good Friday or Christmas Day happened to come in it)
        three times a week.

He was quite indifferent as to the particular kinds of dresses
    That the clergyman wore at the church where he used to go to
        pray,
And whatever he did in the way of relieving a chap's distresses,
    He always did in a nasty, sneaking, underhanded, hole-and-
        corner sort of way.

I have known him indulge in profane, ungentlemanly emphatics,
    When the Protestant Church has been divided on the subject of
        the width of a chasuble's hem;
I have even known him to sneer at albs – and as for dalmatics,
    Words can't convey an idea of the contempt he expressed for
        them.

He didn't believe in persons who, not being well off themselves,
        are obliged to confine their charitable exertions to collecting
        money from wealthier people,
    And looked upon individuals of the former class as ecclesiastical
        hawks;
He used to say that he would no more think of interfering with his
        priest's robes than with his church or his steeple,
    And that he did not consider his soul imperilled because some-
        body over whom he had no influence whatever, chose to
        dress himself up like an ecclesiastical Guy Fawkes.

This shocking old vagabond was so unutterably shameless
    That he actually went a-courting a very respectable and pious
        middle-aged sister, by the name of Biggs:
She was a rather attractive widow whose life, as such, had always
        been particularly blameless;
    Her first husband had left her a secure but moderate competence
        owing to some fortunate speculations in the matter of figs.

She was an excellent person in every way – and won the respect
        even of Mrs Grundy,
    She was a good housewife, too, and wouldn't have wasted a
        penny if she had owned the Koh-i-noor;
She was just as strict as he was lax in her observance of Sunday,
    And being a good economist, and charitable besides, she took all
        the bones and cold potatoes and broken pie-crusts and
        candle-ends (when she had quite done with them), and
        made them into an excellent soup for the deserving poor.

I am sorry to say that she rather took to Blake – that outcast of
society;
 And when respectable brothers who were fond of her began to
look dubious and to cough,
She would say, 'Oh, my friends, it's because I hope to bring this
poor benighted soul back to virtue and propriety,'
 (And besides, the poor benighted soul, with all his faults, was
uncommonly well off).

And when Mr Blake's dissipated friends called his attention to the
frown or the pout of her,
 Whenever he did anything which appeared to her to savour of an
unmentionable place,
He would say she would be a very decent old girl when all that
nonsense was knocked out of her –
 And his method of knocking it out of her is one that covered him
with disgrace.

She was fond of going to church services four times every Sunday,
and four or five times in the week, and never seemed to
pall of them,
 So he hunted out all the churches within a convenient distance
that had services at different hours, so to speak;
And when he had married her he positively insisted upon their
going to all of them,
 So they contrived to do about twelve churches every Sunday,
and, if they had luck, from twenty-two to twenty-three in
the course of the week.

She was fond of dropping his sovereigns ostentatiously into the
plate, and she liked to see them stand out rather conspicu-
ously against the commonplace half-crowns and shillings.
 So he took her to all the charity sermons, and if by any extra-
ordinary chance there wasn't a charity sermon anywhere, he
would drop a couple of sovereigns (one for him and one for
her) into the poor-box at the door;

And as he always deducted the sums thus given in charity from the
housekeeping money, and the money he allowed her for
her bonnets and frillings,
She soon began to find that even charity, if you allow it to interfere with your personal luxuries, becomes an intolerable
bore.

On Sundays she was always melancholy and anything but good
society,
For that day in her household was a day of sighings and
sobbings and wringing of hands and shaking of heads:
She wouldn't hear of a button being sewn on a glove, because it
was a work neither of necessity nor of piety,
And strictly prohibited her servants from amusing themselves,
or indeed doing anything at all except dusting the drawing-
rooms, cleaning the boots and shoes, cooking the dinner,
waiting generally on the family, and making the beds.

But Blake even went farther than that, and said that, on Sundays
people should do their own works of necessity, and not
delegate them to persons in a menial situation,
So he wouldn't allow his servants to do so much as even answer
a bell.
Here he is making his wife carry up the water for her bath to the
second floor, much against her inclination –
And why in the world the gentleman who illustrates these ballads
has put him into a cocked hat is more than I can tell.

After about three months of this sort of thing, taking the smooth
with the rough of it
(Blacking her own boots and peeling her own potatoes was not
her notion of connubial bliss),

Mrs Blake began to find that she had pretty nearly had enough of it,
    And came, in course of time, to think that Blake's own original
    line of conduct wasn't so much amiss.

And now that wicked person – that detestable sinner ('Belial Blake'
    his friends and well-wishers call him for his atrocities),
    And his poor deluded victim whom all her Christian brothers
    dislike and pity so,
Go to the parish church only on Sunday morning and afternoon
    and occasionally on a week-day, and spend their evenings
    in connubial fondlings and affectionate reciprocities,
    And I should like to know where in the world (or rather out of
    it) they expect to go!

W. S. GILBERT

Matrimony

'Matrimony – Advertiser would like to hear from well-educated Protestant
lady, under thirty, fair, with view to above, who would have no objection
to work Remington typewriter, at home. Enclose photo. T.99 this office.' –
Cork newspaper

> T.99 would gladly hear
>   From one whose years are few,
> A maid whose doctrines are severe,
>   Of Presbyterian blue,
> Also – with view to the above –
>   Her photo he would see,
> And trusts that she may live and love
>   His Protestant to be!
> But ere the sacred rites are done
>   (And by no priest of Rome)
> He'd ask if she a Remington
>   Typewriter works – at home?

If she have no objections to
   This task, and if her hair –
In keeping with her eyes of blue –
   Be delicately fair,
Ah, *then*, let her a photo send
   Of all her charms divine,
To him who rests her faithful friend,
   Her own T.99.

ANDREW LANG

My Parasite

Awhile ago, when sore opprest
With parlous noises on the chest,
I heard some lunatic suggest
   That for a simple cure
A porous Plaster, clapped upon the breast
   Was cheap and sure.

This garment I made haste to don;
And truly, ere a week had gone,
It wrought a magic spell upon
   The megrims and the cough;
The only trouble is that now it's on
   It won't come off.

I've tried the corners first – in vain;
I've tried against and with the grain
Day after day, and suffered pain
   Enough for any six;
I say I've worked it till I've roared again,
   But there it sticks.

It may be that one ought to feel
The pathos of its mute appeal;
I grant that in its dog-like zeal
    The creature far transcends
The love of brothers – ay, and sticks a deal
    Closer than friends.

Still, even then, enough's a feast;
Besides, the poor devoted beast
Is getting shabby, frayed, and creased;
    And, though it doesn't show,
It really isn't nice, to say the least!
    Far from it! No.

But there it is; and means to stay
Apparently till judgement-day
And doubtless when I'm old and grey
    The thing will yet be there;
Soap doesn't seem to make it go away,
    No more does prayer.

P.S. – I've just been pained to read
That, when the hour has come to speed
The parting guest, you merely need
    A strong, determined clutch;
Then give a few sharp jerks, and – oh! –
    In-deed! –
Thanks very much!

                    J. S. KENDALL (DUM-DUM)

Saving a Train

'Twas in the year of 1869, and on the 19th of November,
Which the people in Southern Germany will long remember,
The great rain-storm which for twenty hours did pour down,
That the rivers were overflowed and petty streams all around.

The rain fell in such torrents as had never been seen before,
That it seemed like a second deluge, the mighty torrents' roar,
At nine o'clock at night the storm did rage and moan,
When Carl Springel set out on his crutches all alone –

From the handsome little hut in which he dwelt,
With some food to his father, for whom he greatly felt,
Who was watching at the railway bridge,
Which was built upon a perpendicular rocky ridge.

The bridge was composed of iron and wooden blocks,
And crossed o'er the Devil's Gulch, an immense cleft of rocks,
Two hundred feet wide and one hundred and fifty feet deep,
And enough to make one's flesh to creep.

Far beneath the bridge a mountain-stream did boil and rumble,
And on that night did madly toss and tumble;
Oh! it must have been an awful sight
To see the great cataract falling from such a height.

It was the duty of Carl's father to watch the bridge on stormy
                    nights,
And warn the on-coming trains of danger with the red lights;
So, on this stormy night, the boy Carl hobbled along
Slowly and fearlessly upon his crutches, because he wasn't strong.

He struggled on manfully with all his might
Through the fearful darkness of the night,
And half-blinded by the heavy rain,
But still resolved the bridge to gain.

But, when within one hundred yards of the bridge, it gave way
        with an awful crash,
And fell into the roaring flood below, and made a fearful splash,
Which rose high above the din of the storm,
The like brave Carl never heard since he was born.

Then father! father! cried Carl in his loudest tone,
Father! father! he shouted again in very pitiful moans;
But no answering voice did reply,
Which caused him to heave a deep-fetched sigh.

And now to brave Carl the truth was clear
That he had lost his father dear,
And he cried, My poor father's lost, and cannot be found;
He's gone down with the bridge, and has been drowned.

But he resolves to save the on-coming train,
So every nerve and muscle he does strain,
And he trudges along dauntlessly on his crutches,
And tenaciously to them he clutches.

And just in time he reaches his father's car
To save the on-coming train from afar,
So he seizes the red light, and swings it round,
And cries with all his might, The bridge is down! The bridge is
        down!

So forward his father's car he drives,
Determined to save the passengers' lives,
Struggling hard with might and main,
Hoping his struggle won't prove in vain.

And so on comes the iron-horse, snorting and rumbling,
And the mountain-torrent at the bridge kept roaring and tumbling;
While brave Carl keeps shouting, The bridge is down! The bridge
    is down!
He cried with a pitiful wail and sound.

But, thank heaven, the engine-driver sees the red light
That Carl keeps swinging round his head with all his might;
But bang! bang! goes the engine with a terrible crash,
And the car is dashed all to smash.

But the breaking of the car stops the train,
And poor Carl's struggle is not in vain;
But, poor soul, he was found stark dead,
Crushed and mangled from foot to head!

And the passengers were all loud in Carl's praise,
And from the cold wet ground they did him raise,
And tears for brave Carl fell silently around,
Because he had saved two hundred passengers from being drowned.

In a quiet village cemetery he now sleeps among the silent dead,
In the south of Germany, with a tombstone at his head,
Erected by the passengers he saved in the train,
And which to his memory will long remain.

WILLIAM MCGONAGALL

Elsie Gloy

A POEM OF INNOCENCE

She dwelt among the untrodden ways
   Beside the river Wandle;
A maiden, in those early days,
Whom there were very few to praise,
   And fewer still to fondle.
She had a rustic woodland air
That was extremely hard to bear.

Oft had I heard of Canon Gloy,
   And, by the Wandle Water,
Where I went poaching as a boy,
I used to gaze with secret joy
   Upon his seventh daughter;
And while her father was in church,
She helped me snare the local perch.

How sweet it was to watch her swim!
   What fullness of perfection!
So blithe she was, so lithe of limb,
Each primrose by the river's brim
   Reflected her complexion.
So gracefully she splashed about;
She was, indeed, a perfect trout.

No minnow sporting in the stream
   Was half so deft or agile!
Fit subject for a poet's theme!
I looked on her as Love's Young Bream
   Alas! she proved as fragile!
A human pike arrived, one day
And whirled my little dace away!

An artist he, in velvet cape,
    With palette, oils and brushes,
Who wished to paint an aquascape
And, noticing a female shape
    Entangled in the rushes,
He came to ask what he had found
That was so large and smooth and round.

'It is Miss Elsie Gloy,' I said,
In accents somewhat scathing.
'Then, do you think,' he cried, 'instead
Of posing on the river-bed
    As Amphitrite bathing,
She would consent to sit to me
As Venus rising from the sea?'

A snake had entered Paradise!
    The maiden, all unwitting,
Regardless of my good advice,
Consented once – nay, even twice –
    To give the man a sitting.
The love she bore for *me* grew dim,
But oh! the deference to *him!*

She posed each day from ten till four
    (With half an hour to rest in),
And though I could not but deplore
The scanty garments that she wore,
    These sessions so clandestine
Supplied him with the atmosphere
To paint 'the picture of the year'.

*

Now Canon Gloy had got a friend,
    A famed Academician,
Who always asked him up to spend

A night in London to attend
    That Summer Exhibition
Where artists (and some others too)
Expose their wares to public view.

So off to town the Canon went,
    To view the season's pictures.
His gaze on catalogues he bent;
Some portraits he would compliment,
    On others he passed strictures;
No single canvas did he miss
Till suddenly – ah, what was this?

This daub, enskied beneath the dome,
    How pagan, how immoral!
'Venus Emergent from the Foam',
Arrayed in sea-weed and a comb,
    Two crayfish and some coral –
As shyly from the frame she smiled,
He recognized his seventh child!

'O Death,' he cried, 'where is thy sting?'
    He staggered like a drunkard.
'An enemy hath done this thing!
Oh, hark the herald angels sing!'
    He was completely bunkered.
He had a stroke, I understand
(Which left him still with two in hand).

'Show me the gay Lothario
    Who's compromised my Elsie!'
He left the crowded picture-show,
And sought the painter's studio
    In Cheyne Gardens, Chelsea;
And there he found the dirty dog
He'd spotted in the catalogue.

'Thou wilting snail!' the Canon raved
  (Misquoting from the Psalter),
'Though scurvily thou has behaved,
My daughter's honour must be saved!
    Go, lead her to the altar!'
The painter answered: 'All serene!
So long, and toodle-oo, old Dean!'

So, in the Chapel called Savoy,
    He purged his grave offences
By marrying Miss Elsie Gloy
Whose services he could employ
    To lessen his expenses.
No other model did he need;
She proved a model wife indeed!

She loved to pose (with little on)
    As Jezebel or Circe,
As Leda (with attendant swan),
Antaea (with Bellerophon)
    Or Beldam (without Mercy),
While, as Europa (with a Bull),
Her cup of joy was nearly full.

Supreme in Chelsea now she reigns,
    The centre of a *salon*,
Surrounded by a herd of swains,
And if perchance her spouse complains
    She merely answers: 'Allons!
La vie est brève; un peu de fun
Un peu de rève, et puis c'est done!'

That is the life she loves to lead,
    As Queen of all Bohemia.
Her courtiers may belong, indeed,
To what is called the 'Wildflow'r' breed,

And suffer from anaemia,
But still her heart with pleasure thrills
When dancing with those daffodils.

Her 'cocktail parties' all adore.
      The more excited *she* grows,
Reclining cross-legged on the floor,
The more her guests delight to roar
      Like spiritual negroes,
Declaiming that the sons of God
Are always adequately shod.

Although her voice is much inclined
      To wander off the note, she
Will oft let joy be unrefined
(Especially when she has dined)
      And render, *blotto voce*,
Plucking her ukelele strings,
Such songs as 'If my worms had wings!'

Like some Bacchante, sitting there –
      Some rustic, pagan goddess –
Her sandalled feet are blonde and bare,
Last night's dessert is in her hair,
      And while her ample bodice
Is decked with moss or edelweiss,
Her skirt is trimmed with corn and mice.

*

Ah, me! By Wandle waters now
      I roam in deepest dudgeon.
I wander lonely as a cow,
For there is none to show me how
      To snare the smallest gudgeon.
I'm left with naught but eggs to poach,
A knight *sans* perch *et sans* (rep) roach!

HARRY GRAHAM

The Mouse-Trap

1

Palmström is very ill at ease:
He has a mouse, but has no cheese.

Korf, answering his heart's desire,
Builds him a cabinet of wire,

And with a fine-toned violin
He sets his boon companion in.

The night descends, the dog-stars bark.
Palmström makes music in the dark.

And while the sweet strains come and go
The mouse comes walking on tip-toe.

No sooner in than from aloft
The gateway drops down, secret-soft.

Half-hidden in the shadows deep
Sinks Palmström's figure wrapped in sleep.

2

Next morning Korf, with gloves and gaiters,
Loads this elaborate apparatus

(Complete, that is, with mouse and man)
On to a strong removals van

Which powerful horses bear apace
Towards a distant woodland place.

Here, in the leafy silence, he
Sets this unusual couple free.

The mouse trots out to take the air
With Palmström bringing up the rear.

She looks once at her chaperone,
Then wags her whiskers and is gone.

Their task achieved the happy twain
Immediately go home again.

CHRISTIAN MORGENSTERN
(translated R. F. C. HULL)

Tibetan Lament

The loveliest of our lamas
Is gone beyond the door.
He'll never wear pyjamas
Any more, any more.

Above the yawning chasm
He tried to pass a yak;
It took a sneezing spasm
And blew him off the track.
Now the silent valley has him,
And he can't come back.

The loveliest of our lamas
Is gone beyond the door.
He'll never wear pyjamas
Any more.

J. B. NAISMITH

The Bishop's Mistake

The bishop glanced through his window pane
On a world of sleet, and wind, and rain,
When a dreary figure met his eyes
That made the bishop soliloquize.

And as the bishop gloomily thought
He ordered pen and ink to be brought,
Then 'Providence Watches' he plainly wrote
And pinned the remark to a ten bob note.

Seizing his hat from his lordly rack
And wrapping his cloak around his back,
Across the road the bishop ran
And gave the note to the shabby man.

That afternoon was the bishop's 'at home'
When everyone gathered beneath his dome,
Curate and canon from far and near
Came to partake of the bishop's cheer.

There in the good old bishop's hall
Stood a stranger lean and tall,
'Your winnings, my lord' he cried. 'Well done –
"Providence Watches", at ten to one.'

It is to be noted on Sunday next
The bishop skilfully chose his text,
And from the pulpit earnestly told
Of the fertile seed that returned tenfold.

AUTHOR UNKNOWN

Second Philosopher's Song

If, O my Lesbia, I should commit,
Not fornication, dear, but suicide,
My Thames-blown body (Pliny vouches it)
Would drift face upwards on the oily tide
With the other garbage, till it putrefied.

But you, if all your lovers' frozen hearts
Conspired to send you, desperate, to drown –
Your maiden modesty would float face down,
And men would weep upon your hinder parts.

'Tis the Lord's doing. Marvellous is the plan
By which this best of world's is wisely planned.
One law He made for woman, one for man:
We bow the head and do not understand.

ALDOUS HUXLEY

His Hirsute Suit

A bristling beard was his peculiarity:
    He kissed. She thought it smacked of insincerity,
    And bridling up remarked with great severity,
'Such misdemeanors are, I trust, a rarity;
Also your face, despite its angularity,
    Is hidden in a razorless asperity:
    Were it not so, I call it great temerity –
Our walks in life are not upon a parity.'

Wherefore he shaved, to give his chin the purity
　　It knew ere he emerged from his minority.
The razor, naked, with no guard's security,
　　Slipped. Gizzard cut, he joined the great majority.
Where he will pass the aeons of futurity –
Above – below – I can't say with authority.

F. SIDGWICK

The Grange

Oh there hasn't been much change
At The Grange.

Of course the blackberries growing closer
Make getting in a bit of a poser
But there hasn't been much change
At The Grange.

Old Sir Prior died
They say on the point of leaving for the seaside
They never found the body which seemed odd to some
(Not me, seeing as what I seen the butler done)

Oh there hasn't been much change
At The Grange.

The governess as got it now
Miss Ursy having moved down to The Green Cow
Seems proper done out of er rights a b. shame
And what's that the governess pushes round at nights in the old pram?

No there hasn't been much change
At The Grange.

The shops leave their stuff at the gates now – meat, groceries
Mostly old canned goods you know from McInnes's
They would't go up to the door,
Not after what happened to Fred's pa.

Oh there hasn't been much change
At The Grange.

Parsing there early this morning, cor lummy,
I hears a whistling sound coming from the old chimney
Whistling it was fit to bust and not a note wrong
The old pot, whistling *The Death of Nelson*.

Oh there hasn't been much change
At The Grange.

But few goes that way somehow
Not now.

                                        STEVIE SMITH

Obituary

Life's little day is fading fast; upon the mountain's brow, the sink-
ing sun is gleaming red: the shadows lengthen now. The twilight
hush comes on apace, and soon the evening star will light us to
those chambers dim where dreamless sleepers are; and when the
curfew bell has rung that calls us all to rest, and we have left all
earthly things at Azrael's request, O may some truthful mourner
rise and say of you or me: 'Gee-whiz! I'm sorry that he's dead: he
was a honey-bee! Whate'er his job, he did his best: he put on all
his steam. In everything he had to do, he was a four-horse team.
He thought that man was placed on earth to help his fellow-guys:
he never wore a frosty face, and balked at weepy eyes. The hard-
luck pilgrim always got a handout at his door; and any friend
could help himself to all he had in store. He tried to make his

humble home the gayest sort of camp, till Death, the king of
bogies, came and slugged him in the lamp. There never was a
squarer guy existed in the land; and Death was surely off his base
when that galoot was canned.

WALT MASON

Notting Hill Polka

We've – had –
A Body in the house
　　Since Father passed away:
He took bad on
Saturday night an' he
　　Went the followin' day:

Mum's – pulled –
The blinds all down
　　An' bought some Sherry Wine,
An' we've put the tin
What the Arsenic's in
　　At the bottom of the Ser-pen-tine!

W. BRIDGES-ADAMS

Birthday Blues

DAISY, PRINCESS OF PLESS, AT KIEL, 1903

Sun-spangled morning! Baltic June!
The yacht is clinically clean,
The summer breeze conveys from Omsk
A breath of ice and evergreen;

Paintwork all white, outside and in,
And pennants flickering like whips,

And jostling ripples keeping up
That slipshod slap against the ships;

Later of course the shadeless deck
Will burn, one's thin-soled shoes will bake –
Can I be twenty-nine today?
Can I? There must be some mistake!

Though fearfully smart, this yachting suit
Did seem the fittest thing to buy,
Neat sailor blouse and short blue skirt,
White shoes, and scarlet cap and tie ...

I wonder if I dress too young?
Do I? I don't know what to think;
Stout hags of forty flaunt and flirt
In frilly tulle and girlish pink;

My figure's perfect, what is *not*
Is that vile figure, TWENTY-NINE!
A birthday if today must be,
Then why, oh *why* need it be *mine?*

WILLIAM PLOMER

I'm a Treble in the Choir

In the Choir I'm a treble
And my singing is the debbel!
I'm a treble in the Choir!
They sing high but I sing higher.
Treble singing's VERY high,
But the highest high am I!
Soon I'll burst like any bubble:
I'm a treble – that's the trouble!

EDMOND KAPP

Defenestration

I once had the honour of meeting a philosopher called McIndoe
Who had once had the honour of being flung out of an upstairs
    window.
During his flight, he said, he commenced an interesting train of
    speculation
On why there happened to be such a word as defenestration.

There is not, he said, a special word for being rolled down a roof
    into a gutter;
There is no verb to describe the action of beating a man to death
    with a putter;
No adjective exists to qualify a man bound to the buffer of the
    12.10 to Ealing,
No abstract noun to mollify a man hung upside down by his
    ankles from the ceiling.

Why, then, of all the possible offences so distressing to humani-
    tarians,
Should this one alone have caught the attention of the verbarians?
I concluded (said McIndoe) that the incidence of logodaedaly was
    purely adventitious.
About a thirtieth of a second later, I landed in a bush that my
    great-aunt brought back from Mauritius.

I am aware (he said) that defenestration is not limited to the
    flinging of men through the window.
On this occasion, however, it was so limited, the object defen-
    estrated being, I, the philosopher, McIndoe.

R. P. LISTER

The Mermaid

Say not the mermaid is a myth,
I knew one once named Mrs Smith.
She stood while playing cards or knitting;
Mermaids are not equipped for sitting.

OGDEN NASH

Assorted Chocolates

If some confectioner were willing
To let the shape announce the filling,
We'd encounter fewer assorted chocs,
Bitten into and returned to the box.

OGDEN NASH

Funebrial Reflection

Among the anthropophagi
One's friends are one's sarcophagi.

OGDEN NASH

The Drummer

He sold his soul
To the Devil he did –
The Devil he did!
For a couple of quid;
And really I think
He was very well rid
Of a soul like his
For a couple of quid.
I honestly think
He properly did
The Devil he did!

MICHAEL FLANDERS

With Every Regret

For many years the undersigned
Has struggled to improve his mind;
He now is mortified and moved
To find it is not much improved.

His unremitting efforts were
To build a sterling character;
The best that he can really claim
Is that it is about the same.

He went through many a tedious drill
Developing the power of will,
The muscles, and the memory.
They're roughly what they used to be.

Alas! the inference is plain
That Education is in vain,
And all the end of our endeavour
Is to be just as dumb as ever.

MORRIS BISHOP

Something Should be Done about the Muses

As if I didn't have enough to worry about,
  I got to worrying about the Muses.
Even their names I was a little blurry about;
  True, they are designations one infrequently uses.

I have no actual quarrel with Clio, Terpsichore,
  Or even Urania, Muse of Astronomy.
It doesn't require any particular trickery
  To fit them into our modern economy.

But Calliope, Muse of Epic Poetry! Who now
 Writes epic poems? They've dropped to their minima!
Only in Hollywood are Epics in view now,
 So let's make Calliope Muse of the Cinema.

And Erato, Muse of Erotic Poetry! Shame
 On Erato and on all those whom her screeds amuse!
Let us, rather, give to Erato an honest name
 As Muse of Television, and by golly it needs a Muse.

MORRIS BISHOP

The Perforated Spirit

The fellows up in Personnel,
 They have a set of cards on me.
The sprinkled perforations tell
 My individuality.

And what am I? I am a chart
 Upon the cards of IBM;
The secret places of the heart
 Have little secrecy for them.

It matters not how I may prate,
 They punch with punishments my scroll.
The files are masters of my fate,
 They are the captains of my soul.

Monday my brain began to buzz;
 I was in agony all night.
I found out what the trouble was:
 They had my paper clip too tight.

MORRIS BISHOP

In Town

I was leaning against the ceiling
As I walked across the wall;
I thought, if the ceiling gives way,
I am in for a nasty fall.

But I screwed my head in place
And buttoned my ears once more,
And continued to walk northeast
Till I came to the parlour floor.

The floor was on top of its carpet,
It looked to me upside down;
But I think my viewpoint is altered
From living too long in town.

CLARK STILLMAN

Women

I like lemon on my salmon,
Some like salmon plain.
It is much the same with women,
By and large and in the main.

If you want a chain reaction,
Leave your chain out in the rain.
It is much the same with women,
By and large and in the main.

Once when I was just a human,
Someone tampered with my brain.
It is much the same with women,
By and large and in the main.

CLARK STILLMAN

Autobiography of an Honest Man

> During the night
> I was out of sight;
> During the day
> I was in the way.

CLARK STILLMAN

Cockles and Mussels

'In the juvenescence of the year'
Came Angela to the seashore,
With Molly Moloney
Dancing on the seashore.

And after them hurrying
And scurrying with hope
Came Big Bill Barnacle
With a long long telescope.

Came Bill with a friend
Who had not been to sea,
A student: a pal
With a Trinity degree.

The story is short
Which I now have to tell,
Molly and Angela
Wished to plunge in the swell.

And undressed on the sands
Thinking no one was near
Among the cockles and mussels
In the juvenescence of the year.

What happened next hour
We'll skip and just say
The tide it swep in
While the four were at play,

And the frocks made for dancing
And the Trinity hose
And the bell bottom trousers
Were devoured by the waves.

The moral I think is
You should never be found
In the juvenescence of the year
Running stark naked around –

Or like Molly and Angela
And B. Barnacle and friend
You may have to get home
Covered only by hand –

And no painterly talent
Within miles to essay
An odd fig leaf or two,
Or a cloud to apply.

EWART MILNE

Adipose Idolatry

The mild Hindoos have household gods
To which they bow each day and night;
But they are not such senseless clods
To celebrate this curious rite,
For I am just as mad as they
Appear – I have a little bust,

A little bust of Thackeray,
And nightly to it in the dust
I bow the head and bend the knee
In strict routine's solemnity.

Myself when young and poor and rash
Discovered William Makepeace T.,
His writings collared all my cash,
Attention, leisure, sympathy.
The world, the flesh, the cares of self,
Time passing, drive our youth away;
But still there stand upon my shelf
The bust and tomes of Thackeray;
And though I rarely read him now
I make him my diurnal bow.

For every night I close my door,
Disrobe myself, and then before
Great Thackeray and all his works
Perform my course of physical jerks.

FRANK ARTHUR

Four Dead Beats to the Bar

While day still was, four dead beats to the bar came there
Wearing their sultry thirsts at a Saturday angle,
Each clothed in melancholy's threadbare mantle
And the bright unenviable medals of despair.

Later they sang: blew bawdy songs from blubbery lips
Like gaudy bubbles, braved the ticking cannonade;
Toasted their toasts, composed a purple serenade
To every maid and bar, to all the whores and hips.

Then thin bells squealed that there must be no light,
No drink, nor any serenading from henceforth;
And four dead beats to a drunken rhythm waltzed
Out to be swallowed by the panting thirsty night.

VERNON SCANNELL

Garbled Gifts

From Florida to the Corinthian Isthmus
People give people gifts for Christmas;
Some give hampers from Mason (and Fortnum)
With the rarest viands that can be bortnum,
Some give a weighty tome of Nietzsche's,
Some give powder, for female fietzsches,
Some give a fascist ham from Eire,
Some knit socks for a well-loved weire –

But some, who were never told what taste meant,
Buy terrible things from the bargain basement,
Things so tasteless that taste is minus,
For well was it said by St Thomas Aquinus
Sicut ens sicut unum, which, construed,
Means a thing is ONE, not a spawn or brood;
Yet people save up for monce and monce
For things that are several things at once –
The electric fire that is shaped like a yacht,
With copper sails round a mast red-hacht,
The fountain-pen-cum-cigarette-lighter
For the busy (and tasteless) smoker-wrighter,
The teapot shaped like a country cottage,
The razor that uses not soap but wattage,
The pourer of whisky, or even wyne,
Which when inverted plays Auld Lang Syne –
Not far removed, to the sensitive soul,
From (horror!) the musical toilet roul. . . .

Dear Reader, if you give things like these
Don't let this verse cause a goodwill-freeze;
The author's not arty, or over-zealous –
It's just that this year has made him jealous
By scoring the tally another notch
When nobody bought him
                  A chiming watch.

PAUL JENNINGS

The Shrew

Once you were gentle and adoring,
As beautiful as a dove about my morning.
I never asked. But all the same you came
And trembling every moment spoke my name.

What's come over you? That now you sulk and pout
And every meeting seems to you so boring?
I have not changed. So need you shout
Or look at me with eyes quite so devouring?

Late as censorious as a judge you've grown.
Be off. You can no longer call my life your own.

LESLIE PAUL

The Delights of a Picnic

You are sitting on stones with rheumaticky bones, and a sandwich
    with egg in is handed you,
Though the yolk, for a cert, drops a blob on your shirt, and as
    non-U the others have branded you;
There are George and his Kate, who arrived rather late, and you
    couldn't set off till they turned up;
Then you couldn't go quick, because Willie felt sick and the ride
    gets him terribly churned up;

There are old Mrs Heath with her spit-and-click teeth, Mum and
        Dad, and the kids, and a Cousin,
And they all sit around on the horrible ground, tongues a-wagging
        nineteen to the dozen;
But you feel very old, or your back is too cold, and long-leggety
        beasties are biting you,
Or you're suffering stings from mosquito-like things that are
        dancing but hardly delighting you;
You are loath to be rude, but you're hating the food, which is
        certainly unsatisfying;
Mainly damp-looking lettuce, which felons in fetters might feed
        on if very near dying;
There is molten ice-cream, which you do not esteem – when you're
        dry there is milk going curdly,
For the tool isn't here that they open the beer with, you've left it
        behind most absurdly;
Then the children get hurt, lie and howl in the dirt, and you shout
        at 'em, smack 'em, and shake 'em,
And you swear that again (*walking* home in the rain) for a picnic
        you never will take 'em!

J. A. LINDON

Not so Gorgeous

Dorothy's drawers are creamy gauze;
    Lil's are long and slack;
Tonia's tights are crocheted whites;
    Jennifer Jane's are black.

Betty's bloomers are slaty grey,
    And she tucks her skirt inside;
Polly's are pink – since yesterday –
    I think she's had them dyed.

Sarah's silks were awf'ly dear –
    The best her mum could get;
And (may I whisper it in your ear?)
    Nancy's knickers are wet!

Sue's are blue, and Prue's are too,
    And little Pam's are sweet;
While naughty Meg has lost a leg,
    And Tilly has torn her seat.

Swanky Maisie's are trimmed with daisies
    And patched with coloured stuffs;
But those on Milly look awful silly –
    They sort of flap their cuffs!

Jill's have frills, and Pat's are plain,
    With a button in case they fall;
And (may I whisper once again?)
    I HAVEN'T A PAIR AT ALL!

J. A. LINDON

La Beldam Sans Directoire

ON THE RECENSION OF THE TELEPHONE DIRECTORY, 1953

Picture me, my dear, alone and
Palely doing whatever one does alone,
Receiving, perhaps, an imaginary message,
Silent – like Cortez – on a telephone.

Emperorwise or clownlike listening
– In my dark glasses – to the nightingale
Threading, no doubt, its song through the sad **heart**
Of Truth reduced to tears amid the ale. . . .

Preferring sorrow to a harvest home:
For now, to save a little L. s. d.,
Truth they compress and distance they compel
Who have retrenched the old Directory.

R. TOLSON

Adieu

The slippered silence of the room
And sunlight on the parquet floor
Warn me, my dear adorable,
We'll not get drunk no more.

You, who were wont to toss your drink
Throat down – as bulls hurl matadors
To threadbare sand – now sip as if
We drank to settle scores.

For hours you ride a pony glass,
Tight-reined, tight-lipped, and jogging slow:
Fallen your gaze once proudly held
And your tall tales lie low.

Cage me a peacock! Let me stand
Cloudlike, reviewing daffodils.
The Leith Police dismisseth uth
– And W. D., and H. O. Wills.

R. TOLSON

The Wider Life

I once was a dull, narrow housewife
    With nothing to talk of at all
But the loves, the frustrations,
The rows, the relations
    Of the woman from over the wall.

But now I've a job, I'm quite different;
    I can talk with a sparkle like wine
Of the loves, the frustrations,
The rows, the relations,
    Of the girl at the desk next to mine.

CELIA FREMLIN

A Skimmer of the Popular Press Recalls 1957

This is all that I recall:
    BRIDEGROOM GETS HOT FEET.*
Glumly here I sit and scrawl:
'*This* is all that I recall ...'
Don't know who he was at all,
    Can't explain the heat;
This is ALL that I recall:
    BRIDEGROOM GETS HOT FEET.

R. A. MCKENZIE

* A front-page minor heading in the *Daily Express*, 28.3.57: 'Dreaming happily about his forthcoming marriage in front of the fire, the curious chap didn't notice his shoes were smouldering, and ended up in hospital, wedding postponed I believe.'

Things Alone

A void said to the vacuum,
'cogito ergo sum'.
The vacuum stood up and winced,
and left the place it had not filled,
completely unconvinced.

*

A parasol once in a sunny meadow
tried hard to sit in its own shadow,
but as it moved from place to place,
it said, 'It seems to be the case,
that, quite regardless where I sit,
I never get the benefit.'

*

In a big building lived a lift
which thought, 'I'll cut myself adrift,'
and so it did, while crashing to the ground
it said, 'At last it will be found,
that it is hardly up to me
to fight the law of gravity.'

*

Once a right angle said,
'It's difficult to live along-
side other angles which are wrong.
How often now, that I have tried
to tell them only I am right.
But every time they answer me,
"You take yourself too literally".'

*

A symbol said, 'I represent
the meanings someone else has meant.
I personally have no leanings
towards any of the many meanings.'

*

A line once met another line
and said, 'Well, this is very fine.
Now, that at last you have met me,
we must have reached infinity.'
The other said, 'Oh, this is hell.
We never have been parallel.'

*

'I'm tired turning round myself,'
a roundabout once told the wheel.
'It's silly and a waste of time,
that's what it is I feel.'
The wheel replied, 'I beg to differ,
but possibly you're not aware
whenever I turn round myself,
I always get somewhere.'

*

A drop once said,
'I have a notion,
that I am really the ocean.
The only difference I can see
is just a question of degree.'

HANS HESS

UNSOCIAL COMMENT

On Giles and Joan

Who says that Giles and Joan at discord be?
Th' observing neighbours no such mood can see.
Indeed, poor Giles repents he married ever;
But that his Joan doth too. And Giles would never
By his free-will be in Joan's company;
No more would Joan he should. Giles riseth early
And, having got him out of doors, is glad;
The like is Joan: but turning home is sad;
And so is Joan. Oftimes when Giles doth find
Harsh sights at home, Giles wisheth he were blind;
All this doth Joan: or that his long-yearned life
Were quite outspun; the like wish hath his wife.
The children that he keeps, Giles swears are none
Of his begetting; and so swears his Joan.
In all affection she concurreth still
If now, with man and wife, to will and nill
The self-same things a note of concord be:
I know no couple better can agree.

BEN JONSON

The Fate of Sergeant Thin

Weep for the fate of Sergeant Thin,
    A man of desperate courage was he,
More he rejoiced in the battle's din
    Than in all the mess-room's revelry;
But he died at last of no ugly gash, –
He choked on a hair of his own moustache!

Sergeant Thin was stern and tall,
   And he carried his head with a wonderful air;
He looked like a man who could never fall,
   For devil or don he did not care;
But death soon settled the Sergeant's hash,
He choked on a hair of his own moustache!

Sorely surprised was he to find
   That his life thus hung on a single hair;
Had he been drinking until he grew blind,
   It would have been something more easy to bear;
Or had he been eating a cartload of trash, –
But he choked on a hair of his own moustache!

The news flew quickly along the ranks,
   And the whiskered and bearded grew pale with fright;
It seemed the oddest of all death's pranks,
   To murder a Sergeant by means so slight, –
And vain were a General's state and cash,
If he choked on a hair of his own moustache!

They buried poor Thin when the sun went down,
   His cap and his sword on the coffin lay;
But many a one from the neighbouring town
   Came smilingly up to the sad array, –
For they said with a laughter they could not quash,
That he choked on a hair of his own moustache!

Now every gallant and gay hussar,
   Take warning by this mournful tale, –
It is not only bullet or scar
   That may your elegant form assail;
Be not too bold – be not too rash –
You may choke on a hair of your own moustache!

H. G. BELL

Early Rising

'God bless the man who first invented sleep!'
　　So Sancho Panza said, and so say I:
And bless him, also, that he didn't keep
　　His great discovery to himself; nor try
To make it – as the lucky fellow might –
　　A close monopoly by patent-right!

Yes – bless the man who first invented sleep
　　(I really can't avoid the iteration);
But blast the man, with curses loud and deep,
　　Whate'er the rascal's name, or age, or station,
Who first invented, and went round advising,
That artificial cut-off, – Early Rising!

'Rise with the lark, and with the lark to bed,'
　　Observes some solemn, sentimental owl;
Maxims like these are very cheaply said;
　　But, ere you make yourself a fool or fowl,
Pray just inquire about his rise and fall,
And whether larks have any beds at all!

The time for honest folks to be abed
　　Is in the morning, if I reason right;
And he who cannot keep his precious head
　　Upon his pillow till it's fairly light,
And so enjoy his forty morning winks,
Is up to knavery; or else – he drinks!

Thomson, who sang about the 'Seasons', said
　　It was a glorious thing to *rise* in season;
But then he said it – lying – in his bed,
　　At ten o' clock A.M., – the very reason
He wrote so charmingly. The simple fact is
His preaching wasn't sanctioned by his practice.

'Tis, doubtless, well to be sometimes awake, –
  Awake to duty, and awake to truth, –
But when, alas, a nice review we take
  Of our best deeds and days, we find, in sooth,
The hours that leave the slightest cause to weep
Are those we passed in childhood or asleep!

'Tis beautiful to leave the world awhile
  For the soft visions of the gentle night;
And free, at last, from mortal care or guile,
  To live as only in the angels' sight,
In sleep's sweet realm so cosily shut in,
Where, at the worst, we only *dream* of sin!

So let us sleep, and give the Maker praise.
  I like the lad who, when his father thought
To clip his morning nap by hackneyed phrase
  Of vagrant worm by early songster caught,
Cried, 'Serve him right! – it's not at all surprising;
The worm was punished, sir, for early rising!'

                                        J. G. SAXE

A Dutchman's Dog Story

Dere vhas a leedle vomans once
  Who keept a leedle shtore,
Und had a leedle puppy dog
  Dot shtoodt pefore der door.
Und evfery dime der peoples coom
  He opened vide him's jaw,
    Schnip! Schnap! shoost so,
      Und bite dem.

Vun day anoder puppy dog
 Cooms runnin' down der shtreet,
Oudt of Herr Schneider's sausage-shop,
 Vhere he had shtoled some meat;
Und after him der Schneider man –
 Der vhind vhas not more fleet.
  Whir-r-r! Whist! shoost so,
   Like vinkin!

Der leedle voman's puppy dog
 Vhas lookin' at der fun,
He barkit at der Schneider man,
 Und right pefore him run;
Den fell him down, dot Schneider man,
 Like shooted mit a gun.
  Bang! Crash! shoost so.
   Und voorser.

Der puppy dog dot shtoled der meat,
 Roon'd on and got avhay;
Der leetle voman's puppy dog
 Der Schneider man did slay,
Und make him indo sausages –
 Dot's vot der peoples say.
  Chip! Chop! shoost so.
   Und sell him.

DER MORAL

Der moral is, don't interfere
 Vhen droubles is aroundt;
Der man dot's in der fightin' crowd
 Vhill get hurt I'll be pound.
Mind your own peesness, dot is pest,
 In life she vhill be found.
  Yaw! Yaw! shoost so,
   I pet you.

J. T. BROWN

The Truth about the Cold-Tubber

He had read of the frigid fanatics who tub
   In a pool in the Park through the ice,
So he took a rough towel his body to scrub,
He sped to the Park – quite avoiding the Pub –
     He stripped in a blizzard,
     Which pierced to his gizzard,
And shrivelled his skin till he looked like a lizard,
Plunged, shuddered, shrank, stammered, '*How* n-n-n-n-ice!'
But when through the laurels I happened to glance,
     I found he was – doing the Serpentine Dance,
With a stiff frozen towel, ten paralysed toes,
     And an unripe tomato in place of a nose.

E. J. MILLIKEN

Limited Liability

Some seven men form an Association
   (If possible, all Peers and Baronets),
They start off with a public declaration
   To what extent they mean to pay their debts.
That's called their Capital; if they are wary
   They will not quote it at a sum immense.
The figure's immaterial – it may vary
   From eighteen million down to eighteenpence.
     I should put it rather low;
     The good sense of doing so
   Will be evident at once to any debtor.
     When it's left to you to say
     What amount you mean to pay,
   Why, the lower you can put it at, the better.

They then proceed to trade with all who'll trust 'em,
   Quite irrespective of their capital
(It's shady, but it's sanctified by custom);
   Bank, Railway, Loan, or Panama Canal.
You can't embark on trading too tremendous –
   It's strictly fair, and based on common sense –
If you succeed, your profits are stupendous –
   And if you fail, pop goes your eighteenpence.
      Make the money-spinner spin!
      For you only stand to win,
   And you'll never with dishonesty be twitted.
      For nobody can know,
      To a million or so,
   To what extent your capital's committed!

If you come to grief, and creditors are craving
   (For nothing that is planned by mortal head
Is certain in this Vale of Sorrow – saving
   That one's Liability is Limited) –
Do you suppose that signifies perdition?
   If so you're but a monetary dunce –
You merely file a Winding-Up Petition,
   And start another Company at once!
      Though a Rothschild you may be
      In your own capacity,
   As a Company you've come to utter sorrow –
      But the Liquidators say,
      'Never mind – you needn't pay,'
   So you start another Company tomorrow!

W. S. GILBERT

De Gustibus

I am an unadventurous man,
And always go upon the plan
Of shunning danger where I can.

And so I fail to understand
Why every year a stalwart band
Of tourists go to Switzerland.

And spend their time for several weeks,
With quaking hearts and pallid cheeks,
Scaling abrupt and windy peaks.

In fact, I'm old enough to find
Climbing of almost any kind
Is very little to my mind.

A mountain summit white with snow
Is an attractive sight, I know,
But why not see it *from below?*

Why leave the hospitable plain
And scale Mont Blanc with toil and pain
Merely to scramble down again?

Some men pretend to think it bliss
To clamber up a precipice
Or dangle over an abyss,

To crawl along a mountain side,
Supported by a rope that's tied
– Not too securely – to a guide;

But such pretences, it is clear,
In the aspiring mountaineer
Are usually insincere.

And many a climber, I'll be bound,
Whom scarped and icy crags surround,
Wishes himself on level ground.

So I, for one, do not propose
To cool my comfortable toes
In regions of perpetual snows,

As long as I can take my ease,
Fanned by a soothing southern breeze,
Under the shade of English trees.

And anyone who leaves my share
Of English fields and English air
May take the Alps for all I care!

ST JOHN HANKIN

Sapphics

Really, how these interviews break one's morning!
Barely settled down and I hear a sailor
Been here now for hours – 'have I time to see him?'
        'Yes, I suppose so.'

'Try to tell him something to keep him cheerful.'
'Papers?' 'No! the Registry tried their hardest, –
Can't be found. – They think they're with the Doctors.
        That's where the block is.'

'Well, my man, now why do you keep on coming?
Haven't we said we'll do what we can to help you?
Wrote seven letters, have you? and none been answered
            Save by a postcard.

'Postcard – "case receiving attention" – "printed".
Yes, I know we print it to send out quickly,
But I hope you'll hear from us very shortly,
            Telling you something.

'Quite! it shows the arrears of our correspondence.
Letters should be answered in strict rotation.
Soon as all inquiries have been completed,
            That I assure you.

'I'm afraid I can't tell you more at present;
I'm extremely sorry we've not been able
All at once to turn up your naval papers
            Just for the moment.

'No! not lost. But work in a great Department –
You'd not guess how many we have to deal with –
Means with papers passing between the Sections
            Finding's a long job.'

Well! that's done. The man went away quite cheerful
Talk of 'man's great treasure of hope'! – commend me
Sailors. Yet I fancy I told him nothing –
            Nothing to tell him.

Rather stiff the fare is from east of Poplar.
Gad! I sometimes wonder he wastes his money.
Three times he's been here to my certain knowledge
            All in a fortnight.

Hardly gives us time to fulfil our promise.
Don't quite see why looking at us should make him
Cheerful. I'm not always. And now, confound it!
      Where are his papers?

EDWARD MCCURDY

Sonnet by a Civil Servant to his Love

In th' enforcèd leisure of the hour when tea
   And biscuit sweet (supplied in duplicate)
   The schedules of the mind coördinate,
Some higher rule directs my thoughts to thee.
Then do I register sheer ecstasy
   For thou all lovelinesses integrate
   With charms but too redundant for thy fate
That meets small charm reciprocal in me.

O, might our ways bilateral twine in one,
   And, requisitioning one domicile,
      Share one inclusive, coinciding view!

The teacups' tinkle dies. Once more begun
   The high and changeless round; and here, on file,
      These lines for note and comment passed to you.

ALLAN M. LAING

A Slice of Wedding Cake

Why have such scores of lovely, gifted girls
   Married impossible men?
Simple self-sacrifice may be ruled out,
   And missionary endeavour, nine times out of ten.

Repeat 'impossible men' – not merely rustic,
    Foul-tempered, or depraved
(Dramatic foils chosen to show the world
    How well women behave, and always have behaved).

Impossible men: idle, illiterate,
    Self-pitying, dirty, sly,
For whose appearance even in City parks
    Excuses must be made to casual passers-by.

Has God's supply of tolerable husbands
    Fallen, in fact, so low?
Or do I always over-value woman
    At the expense of man?
            Do I?
                It might be so.

                                ROBERT GRAVES

Hymn

The Church's Restoration
    In eighteen-eighty-three
Has left for contemplation
    Not what there used to be.
How well the ancient woodwork
    Looks round the Rectr'y hall,
Memorial of the good work
    Of him who plann'd it all,

He who took down the pew-ends
    And sold them anywhere
But kindly spared a few ends
    Work'd up into a chair.

O worthy persecution
   Of dust! O hue divine!
O cheerful substitution,
   Thou varnishéd pitch-pine!

Church furnishing! Church furnishing!
   Sing art and crafty praise!
He gave the brass for burnishing,
   He gave the thick red baize,
He gave the new addition,
   Pull'd down the dull old aisle,
– To pave the sweet transition
   He gave th' encaustic tile.

Of marble brown and veinéd
   He did the pulpit make;
He order'd windows stainéd
   Light red and crimson lake.
Sing on, with hymns uproarious,
   Ye humble and aloof,
Look up! and oh how glorious
   He has restored the roof!

JOHN BETJEMAN

The Garden City

O wot ye why in Orchard Way
   The roofs be steep and shelving?
O wot ye what the dwellers say
   In close and garden delving?

'Belike unlike my hearths to yours,
   Yet seemly if unlike them.
Deep green and stalwart be my doors
   With bottle glass to fryke* them.

   * Medieval word for 'deck'.

'Hand-woven be my wefts, hand-made
    My pottery for pottage,
And hoe and mattock, aye, and spade,
    Hang up about my cottage.'

Men of Welwyn! Men of Worth!
    The Health Reform is growing,
With Parsley girdles round the earth
    That recks not of its sowing.

                                    JOHN BETJEMAN

How to get on in Society

Phone for the fish-knives, Norman,
As cook is a little unnerved;
You kiddies have crumpled the serviettes
And I must have things daintily served.

Are the requisites all in the toilet?
The frills round the cutlets can wait
Till the girl has replenished the cruets
And switched on the logs in the grate.

It's ever so close in the lounge dear,
But the vestibule's comfy for tea
And Howard is out riding on horseback,
So do come and take some with me.

Now here is a fork for your pastries,
And do use the couch for your feet;
I know what I wanted to ask you –
Is trifle sufficient for sweet?

Milk and then just as it comes dear?
I'm afraid the preserve's full of stones;
Beg pardon, I'm soiling the doileys
With afternoon tea-cakes and scones.

JOHN BETJEMAN

A Question of Age

LINES WRITTEN AT AN EDUCATIONAL CONFERENCE

'How old are you?' the adult said
Patting the bratling on the head.
The earnest youngster dodged the imminent squeeze,
Patted the adult back, and snapped out 'Please,
Do tell me just precisely what it is you mean;
My age? By birth certificate or by Binet seen?
We cannot with sophisticate intelligence engage
On conversation round this theme of age
When you refuse to make it crystal clear
If you mean Mental, Chronological, or Reading here.
Let us be certain, sir, if we must use a pedagogic term
We use it right, in manner scientific, *juste*, and firm!'
Abashed the untaught adult turned and fled
And wished that ageless child, Methuselah – or even dead.

J. E. MORPURGO

Try it Suns. and Hols.: it's Closed Then

I know a little restaurant
Behind a brownstone stoop
Where *potage du jour* is French
For a can of onion soup.

You order a Martini without an olive in it;
They bring you a Martini, it has an olive in it.
Throw the olive on the floor,
That's what the floor is for.

The tables teem with ladies
Tuned up by Mistress Arden,
And Muzak fills the air
With *In a Persian Garden*.

You order legs of frog, and please omit the garlic;
They bring you legs of frog, all redolent of garlic.
Throw the frogs' legs on the floor,
That's what the floor is for.

The Daiquiris are flowing
Before the meal and after;
The smoke from fifty filter tips
Is shaken by the Schraffter.

You ask them for an ash tray, a receptacle for ashes;
They do not bring an ash tray, instead they bring a menu.
Throw the ashes on the floor,
That's what the floor is for.

I know a little restaurant
Where client and agent grapple,
Where *ananas au kirsch*
Is French for canned pineapple.

You ask them for the check, for *l'addition*, for the bill;
They do not bring the check, they bring another menu.
Throw the menu on the floor,
Walk quickly through the door,
That's what the door is for.

OGDEN NASH

Grin and Bear Left

I don't want to be classed among the pedantics,

But next time I visit friends who have moved to the country I want
to get together with them on terminology, or semantics,

When you ask them on the telephone how to get there they smilingly cry that it is simple,

In fact you can practically see them dimple,

You just drive on Route 402 to Hartley and then bear left a couple
of miles till you cross a stream,

Which they imply is alive with tench, chub, dace, ide, sturgeon,
and bream,

And you go on till you reach the fourth road on the right,

And you can't miss their house because it is on a rise and it is white.

Well, it's a neighbourhood of which you have never been a frequenter,

But you start out on 402 and soon find yourself trying to disen-
tangle Hartley from East Hartley, West Hartley, North and
South Hartley, and Hartley Center,

And you bear left a couple of miles peering through the wind-
shield which is smattered with gnats and midges,

And suddenly the road is alive with bridges,

And your tires begin to scream

As you try to decide which bridge spans a rill, which a run, which
a branch, which a creek, which a brook or river, and which
presumably a stream;

And having passed this test you begin to count roads on the right,
than which no more exhausting test is to be found,

For who is to say which is a road, which a lane, which a driveway,
and which just a place where somebody backed in to turn
around?

But anyhow turning around seems a good idea so there is one thing
I don't know still:

Whether that white house where the cocktails are getting warm and
the dinner cold is on a ridge, a ledge, a knoll, a rise, or a hill.

OGDEN NASH

Ambition

I got pocketed behind 7X-3824;
He was making 65, but I can do a little more.
I crowded him on the curves, but I couldn't get past,
And on the straightaways there was always some truck coming fast.
Then we got to the top of a mile-long incline
And I edged her out to the left, a little over the white line,
And ahead was a long grade with construction at the bottom,
And I said to the wife, 'Now by golly I got'm!'
I bet I did 85 going down the long grade,
And I braked her down hard in front of the barricade,
And I swung in ahead of him and landed fine
Behind 9W-7679.

MORRIS BISHOP

Lines Composed in Fifth Row centre

Of all the kinds of lecturer
    The lecturer I most detest
Is he who finishes a page
    And places it behind the rest.

I much prefer the lecturer
    Who takes the pages as he finishes
And puts them on a mounting pile
    As the original pile diminishes.

But best of all the lecturer
    Who gets his papers in confusion
And prematurely lets escape
    The trumpet-phrase: 'And in conclusion ...'

MORRIS BISHOP

Free From Speech

I said to Dr Wilbur Slade:
'Why do you wear a hearing aid?
Your keenness does not fail, I hope?
You did not need a stethoscope;
You laid your ear on terra firma
And sensed an earthquake out in Burma.
You heard a pin drop in the lobby,
And said: "A safety, not a bobby!"
I grant I am a bit dismayed
To see you wear a hearing aid.'

Said Dr Wilbur Slade to me:
'The apparatus that you see
Is not an Aid, but an Arrester.
I turn the switch; the sorry jester
Recites to deafened ears the wry jest
Culled from the current Reader's Digest.
With this machine I overthrow
The power of public radio.
And with it I need fear no more
The cocktail party's monstrous roar,
The epic of the funny dream,
The arch reproach, the winsome scream,
The tale of How I Earned Success,
The stream of tipsy consciousness.
And chiefly I may now ignore:
"And will there really be a war?" '

'And yet,' I said to Dr Slade,
'Are you not trying to evade
Participation in the fight?
And do you think that this is right?'

A little clicking sound I heard.
'I cannot hear a single word;
Yell if you like,' said Dr Slade.
He patted his Unhearing Aid.

MORRIS BISHOP

Consular and Diplomatic

I rather think the Minister would feel
   Rapprochements of this kind are his affair:
Since he could have me broken on the wheel
   Why don't you sound him? Frankly, I don't dare.

How do you have the impudence to do?
   And what the Devil's your plebeian name?
Legations have no truck with such as you;
   Back to the Consul, sir, from whom you came.

You found him unresponsive? Well, well, well;
   He's bothered – as you know, we're in a mess;
Still, when the Minister says Go to hell,
   You'll understand the Consul can't say less.

You like I work this thing for England's good?
   My wife's Friend can – you pay him buckshee then?
For Dragomans is all one brotherhood:
   So why, O why, you ask those silly men?

W. BRIDGES-ADAMS

A Grotesque

Dr Newman with the crooked pince-nez
Has studied in Vienna and Chicago,
Chess was his only relaxation.
And Dr Newman remained unperturbed
By every nastier manifestation
Of plutodemocratic civilization:
All that was cranky, corny, ill-behaved,
Unnecessary, askew, or orgiastic
Would creep unbidden to his side-door (hidden
Behind a poster in the Tube Station,
Nearly half-way up the moving-stairs),
Push its way in, to squat there undisturbed
Among box-files and tubular steel-chairs.
He was once seen at the Philharmonic Hall
Noting the reactions of two patients,
With pronounced paranoiac tendencies,
To old Dutch music. He appeared to recall
A tin of lozenges in his breast-pocket,
Put his hand confidently in –
And drew out a black imp, or sooterkin,
Six inches long, with one ear upside-down,
Licking at a vanilla ice-cream cornet –
Then put it back again with a slight frown.

ROBERT GRAVES

Miss Multitude at the Trombone

If trombone music be the food of love,
  Play on, Miss Multitude, assuage my hunger,
Nor heed the tale, my brawny turtle-dove,
  Of Mrs Relf, divorced by a fishmonger.
Thou wert not born to burst, immortal bird,
  Though gales of breath may shake thy massive frame.
Heard melodies are sweet; leave those unheard
  To instruments which daintier mouths may tame.
Follow thy vision, laboriously pursued
  From blast to blast. Play on, Miss Multitude.

J. B. MORTON

Mistaken Identity

The smiling film-star stood, to meet
The mob that surged along the street.
Before the man could say a word
They charged him like a maddened herd,
And knocked him down and trampled him,
And almost tore him limb from limb.
Then, laughing wildly through their tears,
They ripped his clothes for souvenirs,
Snatched bits of trouser, strips of shirt,
And left him lying in the dirt.
But one, whose wits were wide awake,
Knew they had made a slight mistake,
And thus addressed the hideous throng:
'Hi! Wait a bit! We've got it wrong!
Oh, damn it all! Take it from me,
He's not the one we came to see.'

J. B. MORTON

The Member for –

Though washed in public, and with great display,
His dirty linen's dirtier every day.

J. B. MORTON

The Liftman

He lives unsociable, aloof,
Between the Basement and the Roof,
Conveying female bourgeoisie
To Sportswear, Hats, or Lingerie.
Devoid of hope, all passion spent,
He travels, glum, pauciloquent,
Without a smile, without a frown,
Just down and up and up and down.

H. A. C. EVANS

Gilbertian Recipe for a Politician

Take a recipe now for that clot of inanity
    Known as the party political man:
From semi-humanity drain off the sanity,
    Dress it in vanity, stuff it with bran;
Add voice like a radio (nobody listening),
    Gobbledegookery, dull as a ditch
(No more to the point than a bull at a christening),
    Droning on – What is he, Labour or which?
The mind of a Marx (it is Groucho I'm thinking of),
Greedy for power that he longs to be stinking of,

Burning to build up an Orwell's Big Brotherland,
Yearning to sit for his portrait (not Sutherland!),
    Form of a Goering – face of a sphinx –
Fond of conferring (to learn what he thinks) –
Leach from these elements all that is soluble,
Toss in a lump of the valueless voluble,
    Pour off the liquid and store it in kegs,
    And a party political man is the *dregs!*

J. A. LINDON

Auto Cyclist

'Twixt those unmann'd
By automobile ease
And he-man pedallers
With hirsute knees
The modern centaur
Steers a middle course,
Half man, half driver –
Helped by half a horse.

MARK BEVAN

To Miss X

AGE 9 OR THEREABOUTS

Some man one day, a better man than I am
    Will look into your eyes and lose his heart,
And quoting, maybe, bits of Omar Khayyam
    Will take you (sans the loaf of bread) apart
'Neath some convenient bough to sing your praises,
    And lover-like, still gazing in your eyes,
Inform you with a fierceness that amazes
    That you are very beautiful and wise.

But could he see you now aged nine or under,
  Your pleasant placid face untouched by care,
Would he not call, with me, on earth to sunder
  And swallow you complete with desk and chair?
Would he not share with me some fellow-feeling
  As I devise, with inward rage, a fate
That may convince you, though it lead to squealing,
  That $5 + 4$ does *not* result in 8!

F. A. V. MADDEN

The Food Fad

Her relatives were all agreed
That very, very large indeed
There loomed in little Ermyntrude
A faddiness about her food.
A puppy dog in half a trice
Will woffle anything that's nice,
And even cats, though more sedate,
Still leave a clean and polished plate,
But Ermyntrude, when she was small,
Could scarce be got to feed at all,
And never, at the table, cared
To eat those edibles prepared.
At breakfast, if her egg were fried,
'Oh, bring me boiled or poached,' she cried,
But boiled or poached, as you may guess,
Would satisfy her even less,
And likewise any other stuff
Received a similar rebuff.
Then, even if her parents hit
On anything she liked a bit,
She shunted it about her plate
And nodged it into such a state

The grisly and revolting sight
Quite robbed them of their appetite.
Each breakfast, therefore, tempers got
On every hand extremely hot,
A really most upsetting way
In which to start upon the day.
When lunch and, later, teatime came
Young Ermyntrude was just the same,
So scenes of violence and of hate
Raged regularly round her plate.

Now food should always, doctors find,
Be eaten with a tranquil mind,
For tums and organs that digest
In these conditions function best,
But otherwise incline to get
Most comprehensively upset.
No wonder then that pa and ma
Grew symptoms of dyspepsia,
And that's a very noted ill
For making tempers badder still.
Hence when one teatime mother said,
'You should, my darling, start with bread
And only after that partake
Of richer things like jam and cake,'
And Ermie thrust her plate aside
And contumaciously replied,
'I'll start my tea with what I like,
Or else I'll – yes, I'll hunger strike!'
Instead of wisely bringing forth
The soft reply that turneth wrath
Both parents gave their anger play
And shouted, 'Right then, strike away!'
And that, so wilful was the kid,
Was just precisely what she did!

The days dragged by and Ermyntrude
Shrank visibly through want of food,
But though her parents sighed a lot
To note how very thin she got,
And urged her, 'Ermie, start with bread,
Do hurry dear, before you're dead,'
They stayed resolved on no pretence
To suffer disobedience,
While Ermie, in her stupid way,
Would rather suffer than obey!

Her weight, when finally she starved,
Was actually more than halved,
Which meant, in coffin and in hearse,
A saving to her parents' purse.
This very clearly shows, or should,
The wind is ill that blows no good.

H. A. FIELD

Trial by Centre Court

Wimbledon. June. Ladies' Singles. Third Round.
Ball-boys abounding all over the ground;
Play started at two, and we're still on the rack.
It's a quarter to five, and they've hardly begun.
A perfect defence meets a perfect attack.
Miss L. Hammerfest meets Miss J. Hunter-Dunn. . . .

GAME TO MISS HUNTER-DUNN. MISS HAMMERFEST LEADS
    BY TWO GAMES TO ONE IN THE THIRD SET, HAVING
    WON THE FIRST BY EIGHTEEN GAMES TO SIXTEEN,
    AND LOST THE SECOND, TWENTY-FIVE—TWENTY-
    SEVEN.

I never liked Tennis.
A damn silly name
With its 'Volleys' and 'Loves' and all that,
The first time I umpired was June thirty-six.
I didn't think much of it then,
I just rather fancied myself in the hat,
Since when
I have umpired again and again and again.
And year after year as I've sat
On court after court,
I've been struck by the thought:
'They are bashing a ball with the gut of a cat.'
What a sport!
You may think it's tedious seen from down there,
It's ludicrous seen from above!

FIFTEEN–LOVE.

Keeping my eye firmly fixed on the ball,
Hoping the linesman will know what to call. ...

FIFTEEN ALL.

As each long-drawn point
Puts my neck out of joint,
What a job!
Set after set!
Oh, the relief when you get
The occasional lob!

THIRTY–FIFTEEN.

What does it all mean?

FORTY–FIFTEEN.

Why 'Thirty–fifteen'? Why 'Forty–fifteen'?
What if instead
I just said:
'One–Nothing, Two–Nothing, Three–Nothing, and Game?'

It'd do just the same.
But some of the older
Debenture-holders
Would be bound to get shirty ...

FORTY—THIRTY.

Now the spectators are trickling out.
There's thunder about,
With luck it'll rain. Oh, what is the use ...

DEUCE.

Five o'clock. Third set. Still only Two-One!
I wish it were dinner.
Thank God – a winner!

ADVANTAGE TO MISS HUNTER-DUNN.

Wimbledon. June. Ladies' Singles. Third Round.
Groundsmen are asked: 'How's the state of the ground?'
Players are photographed jumping the nets,
But here sits a figure one always forgets:
The Umpire upon Whom the Sun never Sets!

MICHAEL FLANDERS

The Crest on the Silver

To every poor relation,
    Where'er his lot be cast,
The annual invitation
    To disinter his past.
The post has brought the flimsy
    Proof-sheets to con with care:
Let us indulge the whimsy
    Of Burke, if not of Hare.

In verbiage monumental
　　Are shrined in tomes immense
Land-owners not so gentle
　　And not-so-landed gents.
Though economic blizzards
　　Distress our noble line,
Let us control our gizzards,
　　And peak, but not re-Pine.

However wide the rift is
　　Between the twig and tree,
Still in the nineteen-fifties
　　Thrives genealogy.
The spark upon the ember
　　Is not extinguished yet:
Haply we may remember,
　　But surely will Debrett.

BERNARD FERGUSSON

Problem

The wind is in the north, the wind
Unfurls its fury at the door;
To turn the cat out seems unkind.

To use him ill I do abhor,
Yet this reflection comes to mind:
Suppose he desecrates the floor?

Though hateful what he'll leave behind,
(To cleanse which were a loathsome chore)
To turn the cat out seems unkind.

He eats a lot, and cries for more:
Roughage, alas, which does not bind:
Suppose he desecrates the floor?

But what if with the dawn I find
Him frozen stiff, and frosted o'er?
To turn the cat out seems unkind.

I'll leave my lino with a score
Of daily journals amply lined:
Suppose he desecrates the floor?
To turn the cat out seems unkind.

                    KENNETH LILLINGTON

Bootless Speculations

One fact eccentric I often muse on:
Girls of sixteen won't keep their shoes on.

Girls, at sixteen, for all our strictures,
Are proper as Puritans,
Pretty as pictures.
With waists cinched tightly,
Wearing ponytails,
They move more lightly
Than a ship with sails,
Than roses shaking
The summer dews off –
But why must they always be taking their shoes off?

Girls of sixteen
Have rows and rows
Of fanciful, lean
Capezios.

Helter-skelter,
To the point of scandal,
Their closets shelter
Slipper and sandal,
Glass shoes, gilt shoes
Shoes with baubles on,
Three-inch-stilt shoes
That everyone wobbles on,
Shoes gone risible,
Shoes for sport,
Shoes without visible
Means of support.
Each maidenly foot is a clad-with-care foot,
But how do they go?
Why, chiefly barefoot.

They never enter
Their entrance halls
But front and centre
The footwear falls:
Pumps under sofas;
Brogues on the stairs;
Loathsome loafers
Beneath wing chairs;
Shoes on the landing,
Lost in flight;
On porches standing
Overnight
While, legs a-taper,
Combing their curls,
Blithely caper
The discalced girls.
Shoeless they chatter their gossip windy
Or barefoot at parties
Dance the Lindy.

For girls, at sixteen, have depths unsounded.
Of sugar and spice
Are they compounded;
Sweetly their powers
Shame doubting Thomases;
They keep late hours
But they keep their promises;
They keep cool heads
For the course they cruise on.
But why in the world can't they keep their shoes on?

PHYLLIS MCGINLEY

In the Swim

No one enjoys more than I do
The pleasures of the swimming-pool, or Lido
When I lie on the concrete bordering this municipal moisture
The world is my oisture.
I do not talk, or read novels of detection,
No, what deep water produces in me is deep reflection;
I am one of the many chaps who
Have only to be at a swimming pool, and they start thinking of the
        primordial ocean, which the Egyptians called Nu and the
        Babylonians Apsu;
Water, says Jung, the sage of Switzerland,
Is an archetype of the Unconscious, from which our Conscious,
        the part that fills in income tax forms, rises in scattered
        peaks or bits o' land.
At swimming pools, when the weather is finer
I dream of broken aqueducts by ruined cities in Asia Minor.
Surrounded by laughing bathers, I am as old as Tiresias or Geron-
        tius
I swim through a green and chlorinated Unconscious,
I love all men –
    but what is this?

Two golden men and a golden miss
Seem to think they're admired by all
For their solemn game with a medicine ball;
They stand in poses we all have seen
On the covers of many a health magazine,
It's clear they think, from their graces and airs,
We wish we could all have bodies like theirs.
Sooner or later they drop their catches,
The wet ball lands on my pipe and matches;
My dreams no longer hatch out from their eggs
When gymnasts trip on my outstretched legs.
The view I take of their sport is dim,
I crossly rise and dive in for a swim –
But here again I am far from solo,
I come up for air in a game of polo ...
Too late! too late! I was just a fool
To think I could dream at a swimming pool.

PAUL JENNINGS

Girl Who Spoke Too Much

Miss Janet Jones had everything
Her father's love and wealth could bring
Except the knack of leading on
The fellow she was sweet upon.
Her doting parents, who aspired
To make her ladylike, had hired
The nicest maids and governesses
To train and comb her mind and tresses.
And from her childhood they had taught
What things are done, what thoughts are thought.
They made her practise prunes and prisms
And shun her father's solecisms,
And lest she blundered had averred
That children should be seen, not heard.

So well were these foundations laid
This very parfait gentle maid
Grew up to harbour more repressions,
Aversions, complexes, obsessions,
And inhibitions and fixations
Than other girls whose educations
Had been the object of less care.

She did not drink or smoke or swear,
And never went a step too far
In anybody's motor-car;
And though the vicar thought her nice,
The vicar's son said, 'Cold as ice.'

Now Janet loved the vicar's son
And wanted to be wooed and won
By him, and was not really cold
As ice at all. She often told
Herself that she would overcome
The shyness that had made her dumb
And caused her to appear to him
So very spinsterish and prim.
She grew quite sick with hopes deferred
Until one night she overheard
A statesman who had come to dine
(Made truthful by her father's wine)
Remark that he was once so shy
He could not even tell a lie,
But when he had become inured
To public speaking that was cured.

'That's good enough for me,' she thought.
So when she found a chance she brought
Herself to tell him she was seeking
To learn the art of public speaking.
'If that's the case, my dear, then go,'

The statesman said, 'to one I know
Who gives instruction, and has taught
A lot of us to air our thought
In words that clarify and please.
And some of them are now M.P.S.
She said she would, and presently
She joined this school of oratory.
Determined to appear her best
She donned her most expensive vest
And Paris frock and silken hose
And spent an hour upon her nose.
She took her father's Morris Eight
And drove up half a minute late
Close to that Palace by the Thames
Whose rafters ring with 'ers' and 'ems'.

Now Janet, though no modern miss,
Had heard of psychoanalysis,
And thought the tutor should have tried
To probe for complexes inside
Her mind, and find some hidden sin
Of hers, or of her kith and kin,
Which may have formed in far-off years
The basis of her doubts and fears.

She hoped, of course, he would not find
A complex that was unrefined
Like some described in books that she
Had once read rather furtively.
But seemingly he was devoid
Of all acquaintanceship with Freud,
And simply said that public speech
Was something well within the reach
Of very nearly everyone,
And really it was quite good fun
(At least for those by whom it's done).

So, unaware of her repressions
She started on her speaking lessons,
And learnt to stand erect and firm
And not to fidget, sway, or squirm,
To open wide her mouth and give
Due weight to very fugitive
Conjunction; not to speak too fast;
To keep her voice up to the last
Word of a phrase and not to drone
In one unbroken monotone.
To gather power by breathing deep,
And when her hearers seemed to sleep
To drop her voice or pause awhile,
Or sit down with a pleasant smile.

She learnt to print her notes on slips
Of paper held by paper clips;
To have those notes but not to need them;
To say her speeches, not to read them.
She learnt that she must keep to time,
That 'ers' were human but a crime,
And learnt what speakers have to do
Who want to put a motion through,
And how bazaars are opened, how
A chairman has to stop a row.

She thought the tutor's 'Excellent'
Was something that he really meant.
She quickly grew from strength to strength
Till confidence arrived. At length
She went along as bold as brass
To practise near the Hyde Park grass
The art of throwing verbal bricks
At rival heads in politics.
Then all her life was changed; she found
No pleasure in the old dull round,

But rushed to meetings in the town,
Put lots of resolutions down,
And found herself a seat on hordes
Of benches, panels, chairs, and boards,
Becoming what the rest might call
The little splinter on them all.
Then one delirious morning she
Was gazetted an O.B.E.,
And thought the honour she had won
Was better than the vicar's son.

Spurred on by that to greater heights
She launched on more ambitious flights.
With money that her father lent
She fought a seat in Parliament.
And as she sat and listened there
She dreamed of social systems where,
As in the worlds of bees and ants,
The women always wore the pants.

At last Miss Janet Jones's name
Was etched upon the roll of fame.
She had the D.B.E., had been
Presented to the King and Queen,
And as she drank no wine or beer
The Lady Astor called her 'dear'.

But yet there was one other honour
That presently was thrust upon her.
A note arrived, a brief request
That she would be the special guest
Of that same school of oratory
Where she acquired the A.B.C.
Of public speech, and would she tell
The school how she had done so well.
She said she would, and in due course
She went, though feeling rather hoarse.

Although excelling in the art
Of speaking, there was still one part
At which she was not very good.
She had not practised as one should
The art of sipping from a glass
To make the – ahem – hoarseness pass.
Her tutor naturally had taught her
How speakers ought to sip their water,
But in the arts of public speech,
However well the teachers teach,
Some public practice is required
Before true grace can be acquired,
And she for fear of losing caste
Had rather funked this in the past.
She thought, 'As I am hoarse tonight
I can repair this oversight
and practise drinking from that glass.
I'm sure the pupils in this class
Will pardon me if by mischance
I do it with inelegance.'

Soon after she began her speech
She stretched a hand across to reach
The glass, and brought it to her lips.
She did it twice and made no slips,
Then kept on practising and deft
-ly drank and drank till none was left.

The speech improved, grew passionate,
Then started to deteriorate,
Trailed off to incoherences,
And then she said, 'Excuse me, please,'
And staggered blindly down the stairs,
Threw off her pompousness and cares,

And other things, went down the road
And in the House of Commons showed
A shocked and gaping audience
How once Salome used to dance.

Well, that's enough; I draw a veil
Across the scene and end my tale,
Except to say the vicar's son
Who really loved this paragon,
But thought she was too proud and haughty
Was pleased to hear she could be naughty
And rushed to woo and wed her then
Before she got high-hat again.

She sought the Chiltern Hundreds and
A little house in Metroland
Where no one knows his neighbour's name,
And there they live unknown to fame.

But Cupid knows the house quite well
And often listens while they tell
How glad they are the liquid in
The tutor's glass was mixed with gin.

LEONARD TAYLOR

The Cocktail Party

'How splendid!' says my host, pressing into my hand
The ice cold glass. 'You know the Bellengers and Will?'
I bow and murmur in mosquito tones: 'How do . . . ?'
The sleek, stout man is like a bird, head cocked, his bill
Intent upon this poor brown worm, but beady eye
Alert for better fare. 'You live in town?' he trills,
And through the clash of drums and cymbals I shout 'Yes!'
Cold on the air a sudden stream my glass refills.

I drink. On Arctic snow there follows leaping flame
And instantly I feel quite determined to sing,
For a whole orchestra of voices is roof high.
But Will has taken off, with scarcely flap of wing,
And offers now a goblet to a pale goose girl.
So I seize a sausage with a cry of pleasure
(Curious, when at home I always avoid them),
Drink from my glass again, essay on Bellenger:

'You are a Londoner?' The thin man nods his head,
Loyally laughing and waiting to add one more
Gay little tale to his shrill wife's about their child.
Turning away, like Will, and fluttering to the door,
'Quite splendid!' I remark, meeting my host by chance,
Wrapped in a scarf of smoke, absently pressing his hand.
Then I float down the stairs alone and into the street,
To pipe my way home. Hooray for a One Man Band!

NANSI PUGH

Double Entente Cordiale

Consider for a moment the French
I mean, of course, the people themselves, not the stench
Of garlic in their underground trains nor their typically Gallic
          morals
Or the way in which their governments govern in a series of awful
          quarrels.
For instance the Frenchman is famous for drinking wine with his
          meals instead of water,
But I think he does this not so much because he likes it as because
          he thinks he oughter.
And also for having small black dogs called 'caniches'
Which if I had my way I would irrevocably banish
Because the caniche doesn't bark it contemptuously mutters
And also is excessively careless on the boulevards and in the gutters.

The Frenchman also has a reputation for designing women's
    clothing
A proceeding which any right-minded Englishman regards with
    loathing,
Because it seems fairly obvious that anyone who spends his time
    concocting things in satin
Can hardly be expected to distinguish himself at bowling or batin.
Which reminds me of another thing which strikes me as curious
And that is why, when Frenchmen play any sort of game, they al-
    ways get absolutely furious,
In fact it is very much more
Like war.
But on the other hand when they really have a war and things get bad
They immediately think they're playing a game and start to cheer
    like mad;
But we should try to get used to the French
Because it would be such an awful wrench
If we had no one to say at the end of a long and successful war, 'Of
    course,
We would have won the whole thing much more quickly without
    the aid of the British Expeditionary Force.'

ALUN GWYNNE JONES

Air for a Plastic Hautboy

'The development of a ruling class, as distinct from a merely monied clique,
is necessary to the Americans. In this development ... heraldry has considerable part to play.'

L. G. Pine, editor of *Burke's Peerage*, in *The Story of Heraldry*

A Wivern Gules for Mr Jones, a Bordure and a Bend Per Fess.
(The Morris Plan called in his loans, and left him armed but
    penniless.)
A gentleman, he lived to fall on
The Field of the Cloth of Orlon.

Three Griffins Or for Mr Brown, engrailed beneath a Crest of
    lawn.
(The National City Bank – Downtown – had warned him he was
    overdrawn.)
Noblesse oblige; he led his file on
The Field of the Cloth of Nylon.

Six Cantons Vert for Mr Smith, with Checky Pales and Trefoils
    satin.
(He died bequeathing to his kith a mortgage held by Chase Man-
    hattan.)
An autocrat, he saved the day on
The Field of the Cloth of Rayon.

But monied, cliquy Mr Bartlett has lost his station in society
(sans Cross Patonce, sans Azure Martlet, sans Pelican in Vorant
    Piety).
He shirked – with funded friends from Akron –
The Field of the Cloth of Dacron.

ROBERT A. KNOWLTON

Cover-Girls

I don't deny you're beautiful
In the extreme, and other places,
But seeing you're identical
In everything (except your faces),
And every page we turn reveals
The same piece (as it were) of stuff,
May I suggest you cover, girls?
You have delighted us long enough.

KENNETH LILLINGTON

The Proper Study

Seated before her window Mrs Jones
Described the passers-by in ringing tones.
'Look,' she would say, 'the girl at Number Three
Has brought her latest boy-friend home to tea;
And, see, the woman at the upstairs flat
Has bought herself another summer hat.'
Her daughter Daphne, filled with deep disgust,
Expostulated 'Mother, really must
You pry upon the neighbours? Don't you know
Gossip is idle, empty-minded, low?'
And Mrs Jones would murmur 'Fancy, dear!
There's Mr Thompson going for his beer.'

Daphne, an earnest girl of twenty-three,
Read Sociology for her degree
And every Saturday she would repair,
Armed with her tutor's latest questionnaire,
To knock on doors, demanding 'Are you wed?
Have you a child? A car? A double bed?'
Poor Mrs Jones would remonstrate each week,
'Daphne, I wonder how you have the cheek.
And then to call me nosey!' Daphne sighed.
'Oh, will you never understand?' she cried.
'Mere curiosity is one thing, Mother:
Social Analysis is quite another.'

— W. S. SLATER

A CLUTCH OF BALLADES

∽

A Ballade of Genuine Concern

A child at Brighton has been left to drown:
  A railway train has jumped the line at Crewe:
I haven't got the change for half-a-crown:
  I can't imagine what on earth to do . . .
  Three bisons have stampeded from the Zoo,
A German fleet has anchored in the Clyde.
  By God the wretched country's up the flue!
– The ice is breaking up on every side.

What! Further news? Rhodesian stocks are down?
  England, my England, can the news be true!
Cannot the Duke be got to come to town?
  Or will not Mr Hooper pull us through?
  And now the Bank is stopping payment too,
The chief cashier has cut his throat and died,
  And Scotland Yard has failed to find a clue:
– The ice is breaking up on every side.

A raging mob inflamed by Charley Brown
  Is tearing up the rails of Waterloo;
They've hanged the Chancellor in wig and gown,
  The Speaker, and the Chief Inspector too!
  Police! Police! Is this the road to Kew?
I can't keep up: my garter's come untied:
  I shall be murdered by the savage crew.
– The ice is breaking up on every side.

ENVOI

  Prince of the Empire, Prince of Timbuctoo,
Prince eight foot round and nearly four foot wide,
  Do try to run a little faster, do.
– The ice is breaking up on every side.

HILAIRE BELLOC

A Ballade of an Impartial Person

'Mr Justice — concurred' – Law Report

They brought in Bills to boil the sea,
   They brought in Bills to burn the town,
To train a cow to climb a tree,
   To teach the fishes how to drown,
   They hanged the Harlequin and Clown
For being knowingly absurd;
   They fined assassins half-a-crown;
And Mr Justice Brown concurred.

They mixed the views of Locke, Legree,
   Burke, Shylock, Cobden, and Calhoun,
They choked the labour of the free
   In yellow mud from Chinatown;
   We broke our blade of clear renown,
We broke our Bank, we broke our word,
   But Britain's statesmen did not frown
And Mr Justice Brown concurred.

Sweet is such antique loyalty,
   Quaint as the rhymes of Ercildoune –
It was decided formally
   By the advisers of the Crown,
   To give to Mr Justice Brown
(Unless a peerage was preferred)
   Say fifteen hundred thousand down –
And Mr Justice Brown concurred.

ENVOI

   Prince, when you spoke in cap and gown,
You let it plainly be inferred
   You thought that 'possum' was a noun –
– And Mr Justice Brown concurred.

G. K. CHESTERTON

A Ballade of Diminishing Control

DIALOGUE OF PASSENGER AND DRIVER

Yes, I admit that Proust is rather good,
  But don't you think old Johnson was a lout?
– Just here the bowmen of King Harold stood –
  Of course I'll stop – it ended in a rout –
  My poor old father passed me on the gout,
I seldom touch a drink or a cigar –
  An admirable inn, beyond a doubt –
What *was* that thing we thought of in the car?

What? One more hostelry? D'you think I could?
  All right! The Spring is here, and one should sprout,
Besides, I see the wines are from the wood –
  If only I were equal to a bout! –
  A small one – no, a large one – the mahout
Of whom I spoke, alas, was drowned in tar –
  It's always thus, the best go up the spout –
What *was* that thing we thought of in the car?

Now, don' you shink you might put up that hood?
  I don' shee why you should ashume that pout –
I only shaid you *might*, not that you *should* –
  Don' be an ash, I shay I didn't shout! –
  Here, mish, my frien' an' me, we want shome shtout –
Shorry, I shought zhis wash zhe private bar –
  Well now, zhe breeding habitsh of zhe trout –
What wash zhat shing we *shought* of in zhe car?

ENVOI

Hi! Here'sh a pub! Put on zhat brake, you tout!
I dunno where zhe bloody hell we are –
  – Yesh! Jush one more before zhey turn ush out –
Wa' wash zhat shing we shought of in zhe car?

J. C. SQUIRE

A Ballade of the Glandular Hypothesis

What hormones had that proud Egyptian Queen?
   And great Napoleon, who had cause to rue
Deficiency of the central endocrine
   Which finally dried up at Waterloo?
   Poor Shelley's optimism was undue,
He never should have dreamed at such a pace,
   He said 'The world's great pace begins anew':
But Shelley had a hyper-thyroid face.

There is a strange secretion flows between
   The interstitial cells; I grant it's true.
It hasn't yet been actually seen
   Not even by the pioneering few;
   Still it will soon be bottled, and on view,
The stuff that made an end of Ilium's race,
   And launched a thousand ships into the blue:
But Shelley had a hyper-thyroid face.

The toad secretes too much adrenalin,
   And drunkards are a thymo-centric crew,
Glandular hyper-functioning has been
   Noted in Florence Nightingale; and you
   Remember Mr Julian Huxley drew
Very strange transformations which took place
   In certain axolotls at the Zoo:
But Shelley had a hyper-thyroid face.

ENVOI

   Prince, let us end our rhymes, they will not do:
Our gonads may be large and full of grace,
   And comely our pituitaries, too –
But Shelley had a hyper-thyroid face.

J. C. SQUIRE

The Impossible Ballade of Whisky & Soda

Sublime beverage, supreme tipple,
　　The slick nectar (but the Haig's slicker!)
Which gods drew from a divine nipple
　　And thick nights became a lot thicker.
　　I'm Pict-Scot, which means a good picker,
I thus drank and through my veins flowed a
　　Benign magic, yes, the true ichor
A large whisky and a small soda.

A full double, or perhaps triple,
　　Descends slowly – feel the sparks flicker
('Twould cure wholly a complete cripple!)
　　And warm cockles of the tired 'ticker'.
　　The world's sick and will be still sicker
Of Krupp, Vickers and the Czech, Skoda,
　　So serve quickly, lest the thugs bicker,
A large whisky and a small soda.

In dark Russia by the Don's ripple
　　They like vodka – the effect's quicker,
But bring Walker and a wee sip'll
　　Convert Malenkov, that dull sticker,
　　And dour Molotov, his side-kicker;
From Kamtchatka to the wide Oder,
　　O let's wish them, with a slight snicker,
A large whisky and a small soda.

ENVOI

　　Beware, Lady, of the dear Vicar,
He's just waiting for the rhyme's coda,
　　He likes ladies and he loves liquor –
A large whisky and a small soda!

                                    H. S. MACKINTOSH

Ballade of Business Consultants

PARTURIENT MONTES, NASCETUR RIDICULUS MUS

'Efficiency!' we cried: 'Let's have them in! –
　　The Hawk-eyed Boys, the "Put-it-Right" Brigade,
Let us expose ourselves, confess our sin
　　(A sort of Oxford Group in terms of trade).'
　　This masochistic urge is dearly paid,
It breaks one's bank and nearly breaks one's heart;
　　We're upside down and gasping for First Aid:
These horrid people have produced a Chart!

Alas, Procrustean Bed! Oh, Loony-Bin
　　Of titles and of hierarchies arrayed,
Wrought by some tortuous-minded Mandarin,
　　Whereto our future fortunes are betrayed:
　　We'll flounder like poor flies in marmalade
Through mazes of Surrealistic Art,
　　Networks of nonsense, grade and retrograde:
These horrid people have produced a Chart.

Stay me with Cointreau! Comfort me with Gin!
　　Here is a game of Snakes and Ladders played
By Groucho Marx and Picasso wherein
　　Heath Robinson himself might be dismayed:
　　The authors of this havoc, young but staid,
Benign and modest, play their baleful part:
　　Sombrely-clad, forsooth, but shod in suède:
These horrid people have produced a Chart.

ENVOI

Prince, you are *dumb*, to call a spade a spade,
Your simple faith has put us in the cart:
　　Top-structure bunkum. . . . Bedlam on parade!
These horrid people have produced a Chart!

H. S. MACKINTOSH

A Ballade of Bereavement

ON LORD WAVELL'S ARRIVAL IN GERMANY WITHOUT HIS
SHAVING-BRUSH

Time was when I was happy and serene
    And mocked at all who thought themselves ill-starred:
Now poltergeists and gremlins intervene
    To haunt and hoist me with my own petard.
    My visit to the Regiment is marred
By a disaster not to be foreseen:
    Timor mortis conturbat, sang the bard –
I left my shaving-brush at Aberdeen.

My morning lather is a might-have-been,
    My shaving-soap is like a lump of lard,
My razor is a mockery (though keen) –
    I might as well have used a Pictish shard.
    The harmony of life is sadly marred,
My face has lost its usual ruddy sheen,
    My stubbled cheeks are cicatriced and scarred –
I left my shaving-brush at Aberdeen.

My chin, once glossy as a nectarine,
    Now looks like holly on a Christmas card,
Or straggly hawthorns in a woodland scene
    Such as is deftly drawn by Fragonard;
    No R.S.M. would pass me for a Guard
However much I titivate and preen.
    My luck would daunt a Roland or Bayard:
I left my shaving-brush at Aberdeen.

*

Pity me, Prince: the water here is hard,
    Hourly my tongue inclines to the obscene,
Full of strange oaths and bearded like the pard
    I left my shaving-brush at Aberdeen.

LORD WAVELL and BERNARD FERGUSSON

Ballade of a Psychiatric Social Worker

They bring me lads who have had their share
   Of trouble in street and meadow and wold.
I try to straighten and set four square
   Young life trampled into the mould.
   How I have sympathized, talked, cajoled –
What they need is a chance to explain –
   But sooner or later when all is told
All my favourites do it again.

What remarkable boys they were!
   Harry the Knife once found and sold
A concrete-mixer on Clacton pier.
   What odd little reefers Chancey rolled!
   And the Strangler's curious Vardon hold!
The Sunday papers are rather a strain,
   Seeing my failures in ten-point bold.
All my favourites do it again.

I said to myself: 'Well, never despair'!
   When Smiler quitted my little fold.
Cured and happy and free as the air,
   He found his railway carriage was cold,
   So, helped by a seventy-six-year-old
Senile delinquent, he wrecked the train;
   Somehow I hadn't the heart to scold;
All my favourites do it again.

ENVOI
   Prince, you have been as good as gold
Since you 'borrowed' that aeroplane.
   You're my reward a thousand fold.
All my *favourites* do it again.

PETER DICKINSON

Ballade of Wishful Thinking 1940

The basic fact about these times of strife
    Is that my job has vanished in the blue.
I've reached another cross-road in my life;
    I'm short of cash (though that is nothing new);
    My hammer-toes have stopped me (sad, but true)
        Joining the army, as had been my plan.
    Right, then, I'll tell you what I want to do ...
        I want to be a Secret Service Man!

I keep my mouth shut, and, when talk is rife
    At parties, I'm the silent fellow who
Sits clam-like near the cocktail-tray. My wife
    Complains that I keep secrets from her, too.
    I am a Sayers-Mason-Lefanu-
        Knox-Oppenheim-Doyle-Buchan-Wallace fan;
    I know an old red herring from a clue.
        I want to be a Secret Service Man!

With practice I could learn to throw a knife,
    And, if forewarned, might manage to construe
The message whistled on a Burmese fife
    Played in a dark, deserted house in Kew.
    I can work out a simple code or two;
        I don't leave letters in the luggage van
    For any foreign countess to go through.
        I want to be a Secret Service Man!

ENVOI

PRINCE, I have lots of push, I promise you,
    And you have pull. Do something if you can
To put me in a job. Er ... *entre nous* ...
    I'd like to be a Secret Service Man.

                        RICHARD USBORNE

Ballade at Eight Bells

IN THE SHIP'S BAR

We spoke of the Equinox. Looking it up,
I found you were off, as you frequently are;
It's the name of a mountain ... The car was a Hup
That your uncle had back in Fort Rockaway ... Far
As I know, you can give it a 't', but it's 'czar'
Which is 'Caesar' spelled 'c-zar'. Here, lend me your pen...
The planets *don't* twinkle. They're closing the bar.
You said it would clear, but it's raining again.

Pourquoi is *por qué*, or *warum* – you know why?
What *is* soup but the sorrow of lentil and leek?
I've mentioned the meaning of mud in your eye;
Now tell me the reason for 'narrow' with 'squeak'.
I thought that would stop you. Remember last week
When you read of Nebraska reversed – Ak-Sar-Ben?
Ak-Sar-Ben? For God's shake, or perhaps for God's sheik,
You said it would clear, but it's raining again.

Why Stamford? The point is they're living in Troy.
Where's the steward? ... All Paris boils down to *Allô!* ...
I can't see a thing ... Say Dram*buie*, not *boy* ...
These portholes all look like an upper-case 'O'.
I'm sure you are wrong; there's no sun deck below ...
A funny name, Shenstone, for what is a shen? ...
It tastes like Old Cree, but he said it's Old Crow.
You said it would clear, but it's raining again.

ENVOI

Prince, perhaps nonsense is all that we talk.
How old is a pullet? How young is a hen?
Who told you Auckland was named for the Auk?
You said it would clear, but it's raining again.

DAVID MCCORD

WORDS, WORDS, WORDS

Three Ghostesses

Three little ghostesses,
Sitting on postesses,
Eating buttered toastesses,
Greasing their fistesses,
Up to their wristesses.
Oh, what beastesses
To make such feastesses!

Old Boniface

Old Boniface he loved good cheer,
    And took his glass of Burton,
And when the nights grew sultry hot
    He slept without a shirt on.

Hokey Pokey

Hokey, pokey, whisky, thum,
How d'you like potatoes done?
Boiled in whiskey, boiled in rum,
Says the King of the Cannibal Islands

I Dunno

I sometimes think I'd rather crow
And be a rooster than to roost
And be a crow. But I dunno.

A rooster he can roost also,
Which don't seem fair when crows can't crow.
Which may help some. Still I dunno.

Crows should be glad of one thing though;
Nobody thinks of eating crow,
While roosters they are good enough
For anyone unless they're tough.

There's lots of tough old roosters though,
And anyway a crow can't crow,
So mebby roosters stand more show.
It looks that way. But I dunno.

A Dream

I dreamed a dream next Tuesday week,
    Beneath the apple-trees;
I thought my eyes were big pork-pies,
    And my nose was Stilton cheese.
The clock struck twenty minutes to six,
    When a frog sat on my knee;
I asked him to lend me eighteenpence
    But he borrowed a shilling of me.

ANON.

Quite a History

'Where have you been, Lysander Pratt?'
'In Greedy Land, Philander Sprat.'
'What did you there to grow so fat?'

'I built myself a little house
In which I lived snug as a mouse.'

'Well, very, very good was that!'
'Not wholly good, Philander Sprat.'
'Now, wherefore not, Lysander Pratt?'

'A bear came raging from the wood
And tumbled down my cottage good.'

'Alas! how very bad was that!'
'Not wholly bad, Philander Sprat.'
'Not bad? Why not, Lysander Pratt?'

'I killed the bear, and of his skin
I made a coat to wrap me in.'

'Well done! Now surely good was that!'
'Yet not so good, Philander Sprat.'
'Now, why not good, Lysander Pratt?'

'A wicked hound tore up my coat
Until it was not worth a groat.'

'Ah, what an evil thing was that!'
'Not wholly bad, Philander Sprat.'
'What good was there, Lysander Pratt?'

'He caught for me a great wild boar,
That made me sausages good store.'

'What luck! How very good was that!'
'Good? Not all good, Philander Sprat.'
'Why not all good, Lysander Pratt?'

'A cat stole in on velvet paw,
And ate them all with greedy maw.'

'Now surely wholly bad was that!'
'Not wholly bad, Philander Sprat.'
'Then tell me why, Lysander Pratt.'

'Of Pussy's fur with silken hair,
I made of gloves a noble pair.'

'Trust you! No wonder you are fat!
You found your good account in that,
As in all else, Lysander Pratt.'

'Yes, in the closet hang they now,
Yet they are full of holes, I vow,

Gnawed by some thievish long-tailed rat;
And so, you see, Philander Sprat,
Not wholly good was even that!'

ARLO BATES

John Day

John Day he was the biggest man
    Of all the coachman-kind,
With back too broad to be conceiv'd
    By any narrow mind.

The very horses knew his weight
    When he was in the rear,
And wish'd his box a Christmas-box
    To come but once a year.

Alas! against the shafts of love
    What armour can avail?
Soon Cupid sent an arrow through
    His scarlet coat of mail.

The bar-maid of the Crown he lov'd,
    From whom he never ranged,
For tho' he changed his horses there,
    His love he never changed.

He thought her fairest of all fares,
  So fondly love prefers;
And often, among twelve outsides,
  Deemed no outside like hers.

One day as she was sitting down
  Beside the porter-pump –
He came, and knelt with all his fat,
  And made an offer plump.

Said she, 'My taste will never learn
  To like so huge a man,
So I must beg you will come here
  As little as you can.'

But still he stoutly urged his suit,
  With vows, and sighs, and tears,
Yet could not pierce her heart, although
  He drove the Dart for years.

In vain he wooed, in vain he sued;
  The maid was cold and proud,
And sent him off to Coventry,
  While on his way to Stroud.

He fretted all the way to Stroud,
  And thence all back to town,
The course of love was never smooth,
  So his went up and down.

At last her coldness made him pine
  To merely bones and skin;
But still he loved like one resolved
  To love through thick and thin.

'Oh, Mary, view my wasted back,
   And see my dwindled calf;
Tho' I have never had a wife,
   I've lost my better half.'

Alas, in vain he still assail'd,
   Her heart withstood the dint;
Though he had carried sixteen stone
   He could not move a flint.

Worn out, at last he made a vow,
   To break his being's link;
For he was so reduced in size
   At nothing could he shrink.

Now some will talk in water's praise,
   And waste a deal of breath,
But John, tho' he drank nothing else –
   He drank himself to death.

The cruel maid that caused his love,
   Found out the fatal close,
For looking in the butt, she saw,
   The butt-end of his woes.

Some say his spirit haunts the Crown,
   But that is only talk,
For after riding all his life,
   His ghost objects to walk.

THOMAS HOOD

Sonnet on Steam

BY AN UNDER-OSTLER

I wish I livd a Thowsen year Ago
Wurking for Sober six and Seven milers
And dubble Stages runnen safe and slo
The Orsis cum in Them days to the Bilers
But Now by meens of Powers of Steem forces
A-turning Coches into Smoakey Kettels
The Bilers seam a Cumming to the Orses
And Helps and naggs Will sune be out of Vittels
Poor Bruits I wunder How we bee to Liv
When sutch a change of Orses is our Faits
No nothink need Be sifted in a Siv
May them Blowd ingins all Blow up their Grates
And Theaves of Oslers crib the Coles and Giv
Their blackgard Hannimuls a Feed of Slaits!

THOMAS HOOD

Prelude to a Second Flood

Once when the world was pink and white
and buxom fairies
danced in dairies,
up a long shadow
in the sun's slant light
walked seventy donkeys
drowsing in their steam,
slow as the sweat of dotards,
ridden by monkeys,
preceded for and aft
by buttoned flunkeys.

The Dowager Countess
of Mulligatawny

lolled in the grandstand,
quizzing a bald trombonist
in a far-off bandstand,
but when this herd
of animals appeared,
she ordered the dead court barber
to a forgotten throne
to trim her short brown beard
for the tufts to be strewn
like flowers before them.

So monsieur le barbier cut his comb
from the cock whence it came,
and on his ten-wheeled tricycle
whirled down the course,
the dandy dame
loping beside him like a roaring river,
but mad for fame
and breathing like a tubed horse.

As the scene flowed by,
he stretched out a hand,
having cocked an eye,
and stole two timeworn scythes
from a green grass yard,
flowering with pea-ripe Aylesburys,
sleek as summer,
spiked them into scissors with a pin,
and turned quick as a stroke strikes.
But the Dowager ducked
then flung herself far
over the tops of trees,
bridges and brimming streams,
past multitudes of minds
cluttered with crimson dreams,
into the Ritz Bar.

The miss complete,
he muttered 'No, no, no!'
called for caparisoned lamas
and left for Panama,
lost in dynastic dramas.

What with the waiters
and her uncut beard,
the Countess distraught,
dying for donkeys
but ordering Martinis,
and nobody around
save Drake and Hawkins,
Madame de Stael and I,
it was a muddled night,
all slapping billows,
for outside
the rain bucketed down
and floods rose to the windows
as though the stars cried.

Crabs were invading houses.
Soles had taken lodgings
in curious places.
The seventy donkeys
had trout in their ears
when they entered the ring
but they ran no races.
For nothing held:
slinking from the filling South
over dissolving dykes
stepped tigers
roaring for another Noah.
Lambs lay with lions.

Great pintpot tears
spilled from full elephants
and quenched old fires.
The raving crowds
were nesting in tall spires
and climbing mountain ranges,
crying 'Safe! Safe! Safe!'
as the waters rose,
but the eels sceptically smiled,
remembering Atlantis
and earlier changes.

J. INGLIS HALL

The Bonehead Bards

The house is mad so am I reading the Bonehead Bards
A donkey's on my window ledge my old man's on the roof
The ass is all of nine feet tall my old man two foot two
And I'm in bed with ten mad poets a wearing verses blue.

My old man he was made of frost the ass was made of snow
And every where that Mary went the ass was sure to go
He followed her to bus one day and met the Bonehead Bards
Is that you Seaumus on the roof if not I'm playing cards.

The ass he chewed the blankets one the ass he chewed them two
The old man pulled him from the ledge and made to make a Moo
I was up the chimney fast and down the shiney roof
And there I met a blessed lass who had an iron hoof.

My old man sat upon the ground the ass was on the bed
The old man said he was a horse a horse was what he said
I'm tired of pull-down moons he said and bones in every line
The ass was quite insulted and the stars fell in the wine.

I'm tired of all them childhoods that one must hears about
Is that the kettle boiling Pa me thinks me hears a shout!
If ever I hear more of bones or moons or darkened souls
I'll boil the poets but one and one and serve them up in bowls.

The ass he was disgusted now he spoke in nine parts greek
And I'm been writing searching poems since Tuesday was a week
I lived with ten green donkeys in the pool of Poolnamoon
And every line contained a bone and every bone a moon.

Lines were short and long-come-short and they could really strike
They were the greatest lines of all I'm sure that you might like
I was the promised bard I was in that unfeeling land
It was at Enniscorty I was forced to take my stand.

They charged at me in waves and out too high in height in all
They came at me with cabbage stumps they swung an iron ball
My handsome tail was reefed in bits I was but torn to shreds
Twas then the fiends attacked me with four six-poster beds.

By starvation boys and nothing more they forced me to withdraw
I eat the cabbage stumps and ran all hurted in the jaw
I've cursed them all a thousand times and best of all that poet
That savage hound who bit my leg and threw me in the moat.

The old man jumped up from the ground and bit the ass's ear
I understand you every word we all speaks greek in here
He pushed him in the moon-faced pot we kept upon the wall
And melted him and melted him till there was not at all.

The house is mad and so am I reading the Bonehead Bards
A goat lies on my window ledge and the great man's on the roof
The Earth is all of two feet tall the great man breaks the stars
Forever chasing Bonehead Bards with great big iron bars.

PATRICK GALVIN

Amo, Amas

Amo, amas,
I love a lass,
As cedar tall and slender;
Sweet cowslip's face
Is her nominative case,
And she's of the feminine gender.
Horum quorum,
Sunt divorum,
Harum, scarum, Divo;
Tag, rag, merry derry, periwig and hatband,
Hic, hoc, harum, genitivo.

JOHN O'KEEFE

The Werewolf

One night an errant Werewolf fled
His wife and child and visited
A village teacher's sepulchre
And begged him: 'Conjugate me, Sir!'

The village teacher then awoke
And standing on his scutcheon spoke
Thus to the beast, who made his seat
With crossed paws at the dead man's feet:

'The Werewolf', said that honest wight,
'The Willwolf – future, am I right?
The Wouldwolf – wolf conditional,
The Beowulf – father of them all!'

These tenses had a pleasing sound,
The Werewolf rolled his eyeballs round,
And begged him, as he'd gone so far,
Add plural to the singular.

The village teacher scratched his head;
He'd never heard of that, he said.
Though there were 'wolves' in packs and swarms,
Of 'were' could be no plural forms!

There Werewolf rose up blind with tears
– He'd had a wife and child for years!
But being ignorant of letters
He went home thankful to his betters.

CHRISTIAN MORGENSTERN
(translated R. F. C. HULL)

Narrative Macaronic Verses

FROM THE BANKOLIDAID, LIB. I

Charmer virumque I sing, Jack plumigeramque Arabellam.
Costermonger erat Jack Jones, asinumque agitabat;
In Covent Garden holus, sprouts vendidit asparagumque.
Vendidit in Circo to the toffs Arabella the donah,
Qua Piccadilly propinquat to Shaftesbury Avenue, flores.

Jam Whitmonday adest; ex Newington Causeway the costers
Erumpunt multi celebrare their annual beano;
Quisque suum billycock habuere et donah ferentes,
Impositique rotis, popularia carmina singing,
Happy with ale omnes – exceptis excipiendis.
Gloomily drives Jack Jones, inconsabilis heros;
No companion habet, solus sine virgine coster.
Per Boro', per Fleet Street, per Strand, sic itur ad 'Empire';

Illinc Coventry Street peragunt in a merry procession,
Qua Piccadilly propinquat to Shaftesbury Avenue tandem
Gloomily Jack vehitur. Sed amet qui never amavit!
En! subito fugiunt dark thoughts; Arabella videtur.
Quum subit ullius 'pulcherrima bloomin' imago,
Corde juvat Jack Jones; exclamat loudly 'What oh, there!'
Maiden ait 'Deus, ecce deus!' floresque relinquit.
Post asinum sedet illa; petunt Welsh Harp prope Hendon.

O fons Brent Reservoir! recubans sub tegmine brolli,
Brachia complexus (yum, yum!) Jack kissed Arabella;
'Garn' ait illa rubens, et 'Garn' reboatur ab Echo;
Propositique tenax Jack 'Swelp me lummy, I loves yer.'
Hinc illae lacrimae; 'Jest one!' et 'Saucy, give over.'

Tempora jam mutantur, et hats; caligine cinctus
Oscula Jones iterat, mokoque immitit habenas.
Concertina manu sixteen discrimina vocum
Obliquitur; cantant (ne saevi, magne policeman)
Noctem in Old Kent Road. Sic transit gloria Monday.

F. SIDGWICK

A Macaronic Poem

'The Kaiser spoke at length with the Baron de Haulleville, Director of the
Congo Museum in French, German, and English.' —

Newspaper report 1910 (?)

Guten Morgen, mon ami,
    Heute ist es schönes Wetter!
Charmé de vous voir içi!
    Never saw you looking better!

Hoffentlich que la Baronne,
  So entzückend et so pleasant,
Ist in Brussels cet automne:
  Combien wünsch' ich she were present!

Und die Kinder, how are they?
  Ont-ils eu la rougeole lately?
Sind sie avec vous today?
  J'aimerais les treffen greatly.

Ich muss chercher mon hôtel.
  What a charming Schwätzerei, Sir!
Lebe wohl! adieu! Farewell!
  Vive le Congo! Hoch dem Kaiser!

H. G.

To a Friend Studying German

  Si liceret te amare
  Ad Suevorum magnum mare,
  Sponsam te perducerem.
'Tristicia Amorosa', *Frau Aventiure*, J. V. von Scheffel

Will'st dou learn die deutsche Sprache?
  Denn set it on your card
Dat all the nouns have shenders
  Und de shenders all are hard,
Dere ish also dings called pronoms,
  Vitch id's shoost ash vell to know;
Boot ach! de verbs or time-words –
  Dey'll work you bitter woe.

Will'st dou learn de deutsche Sprache?
 Dann you allatag moost go
To sinfonies, sonatas,
 Or an oratorio.
Vhen you dinks you knows 'pout musik,
 More ash any other man,
Be sure de soul of Deutschland
 Into your soul is ran.

Will'st dou learn de deutsche Sprache?
 Dou moost eat apout a peck
A week, of stinging sauerkraut,
 Und sefen pfoundts of speck,
Mit Gott knows vot in vinegar,
 Und deuce knows vot in rum:
Dis ish de only cerdain vay
 To make de accents coom.

Will'st dou learn de deutsche Sprache?
 Brepare dein soul to shtand
Soosh sendences ash ne'er vas heardt
 In any oder land.
Till dou canst make parentheses
 Intwisted – ohne zahl –
Dann wirst du erst deutschfertig seyn,
 For a languashe ideál.

Willst dou learn de deutsche Sprache?
 Du must mitout an fear
Trink afery tay an gallon dry,
 Of foamin Sherman bier.
Und de more you trinks, pe certain,
 More Deutsch you'll surely pe;
For Gambrinus ish de Emperor
 Of de whole of Germany.

Will'st dou learn de deutsche Sprache?
    Be sholly, brav, und treu,
For dat veller ish kein Deutscher
    Who ish not a sholly poy.
Find out vot means Gemüthlichkeit,
    Und do it mitout fail,
In Sang und Klang dein Lebenlang
    A brick – ganz kreuzfidél.

Will'st dou learn de deutsche Sprache?
    If a shendleman dou art,
Denn shtrike right indo Deutschland,
    Und get a schveetes heart.
From Schwabenland or Sachsen
    Vhere now dis writer pees;
Und de bretty girls all wachsen
    Shoost like aepples on de drees.

Boot if dou bee'st a laty
    Denn on de oder hand,
Take a blonde moustachioed lofer
    In de vine green Sherman land.
Und if you shoost kit married
    (Vood mit vood soon makes a vire),
You'll learn to sprechen Deutsch mein kind
    Ash fast ash you tesire.

                                    C. G. LELAND

Gaudeamus and Igitur

Gaudeamus and Igitur
Were Romans inseparably.
Where Gaudeamus was wont to be,
He was wont with Igitur.

Never a night were the two at home,
Gaudeamus and Igitur;
It was Gaudeamus and Igitur
In the brightest spots of Rome.

Gaudeamus got gravel soon,
And gout got Igitur.
But 'Gaudeamus Igitur' –
The boys are still the tune.

CLARK STILLMAN

A Charm Against Indigestion

Absit ventus circum cor,
Likewise epigastric sore;
Absit dolor in jejuno,
Which, post prandium, not a few know;
Absit atrox vomitus
With its horrid sonitus;
Absit tum insomnia:
Bismuth vincit omnia.

H. A. C. EVANS

J'ai peur
Du Flu!
Toute à l'heure
J'ai bu
Un peu trop
D'whisky chaud,
Et j'ai vu
Trois faces
Dans la glace:

Trois 'moi'
À la fois;
Et – ma foi,
Tous les trois
Étaient moi!
J'ai peur
Du Flu!

ANON.

Ein Complaint

Herr Direktor, ich sent Sie ein cable,
   zu frag' if some Dinge of mein
in ein drawer in der Ankleide table
   gefunden sind. Ja oder nein?

Ein wunderschön Paar Underpanten;
   ein Nachtgown von Satin gemacht;
und zwei kleine jade Elephanten,
   mein Mann von der Ost mir gebracht.

Und auch, Herr Direktor, ich dinks
   dass ein Taschentuch shpotted mit green
war left in ein Stuhl on die links
   of die Lounge bei das photo of Wien.

Ich cabled der Tag before gestern:
   Warum kommst es nothing dabei?
Ich bitte Sie machen Ihr bestern
   zu schicken mir etwas reply!

VIRGINIA GRAHAM

Pour Ne Pas Encourager Les Autres

J'ai appris beaucoup de français à l'école,
Mais parce que j'ai la tête molle
Qu'est-ce que je m'en souviens?
Rien!
Hab' auch die Sprache Hitlers zu meinem Diener gemacht:
Ich kämpft' es mit dem Führer aus, *Mein Kampf* war meine
    Schlacht;
Leider kann ich mich mit Seiner Honigsüssen Hoheit nicht mehr
    messen –
Alles vergessen!
Conocía a un hombre que hablaba español, era yo!
Trovavo facile l'italiano, ma ci ricorro adesso? No!
See, thou aspiring polyglot, day by day I know less!
Sum quod eris, fui quod es.

J. A. LINDON

Revenants

¿ Quién exhuma
a María
y la pluma
de mi tía?

Nicht mehr Knabe
(Sack von Leder),
sieh! ich habe
noch die Feder!

Femme de brume,
elle me hante –
c'est la plume
de ma tante!

J. A. LINDON

Two French Limericks

Il était un gendarme à Nanteuil,
Qui n'avait qu'une dent et qu'un œil;
   Mais cet œil solitaire
   Était plein de mystère,
Cette dent d'importance et d'orgueil.

Un vieux duc (le meilleur des époux)
Demanda, en lui tâtant le pouls,
   A sa vieille duchesse,
   Qu'un vieux catarrhe oppresse:
'Et ton thé, t'a-t-il ôté ta toux?'

GEORGE DU MAURIER

The Metric System Defied

Some talk of millimetres and some of kilogrammes,
And some of decilitres to measure beer and drams;
But I'm a British Workman, too old to go to school,
So by *pounds* I'll eat, and by *quarts* I'll drink,
And I'll work by my *three-foot* rule.

JOHN RANKINE

Poetico-Mathematical Formula for Success in Love

'Let x denote beauty – y manners well bred,
Z fortune (this last is essential).
Let L stand for love,' our philosopher said,
'Then L is a function of x, y, and z,
Of the kind that is known as potential.

'Now integrate L with respect to dt
(t standing for time and persuasion),
Then between proper limits 'tis easy to see
That the definite integral *Marriage* must be
– A very concise demonstration!'

JOHN RANKINE

Krwelti Tw Children

A FROLLICK

Mai hart iz sad for littel wunz
   Hw uend dheir uai tw skwl
Tw lern dhe Inglish speling uith
   Itz total lak ov rwl.

Dhe aiern enterz taini soulz
   And dhei lwz awl dheir bauns
In lerning werds dhei kannot spel
   And spelz dhei kan't pronauns.

Nau aut upon dhe Parliment
   Dhat thuortid children'z blis,
Prifering prezent drudgeri
   Two luvli stuf laik dhis!

ALLAN M. LAING

Pot-and-Pan and Trouble-and-Strife go Turnip-Topping

One day when I'd washed my old Jem Mace
   and combed my Barnet Fair,
My trouble-and-strife said what about
   a spot of the old grey mare?

Says I: It isn't a ball-of-chalk
    on which your mind is bent:
You're out for a day in the turnip-tops;
    so we'll borrow the Duke of Kent.

She bought herself some daisy roots
    and me a Peckham Rye,
Then a tit-for-tat, wiv fevvers, made
    a hole in me houses-sky.

Just past the Joan of Arc we scoffed
    a cup of you-and-me,
With a once-or-twice of Sexton Blake,
    in a nice little A.B.C.

Then out again on our plates-of-meat,
    spending the bees-and-honey,
She made me wait at the Rory O'Mores
    and seemed to think it funny!

But in a lark-and-linnet I
    shewed who was her heap-of-coke;
For when she fancies some almond-rocks,
    says I: I'm heart-of-oak.

ALLAN M. LAING

Jargon-Jingle

Tawdery! – faddery! – Feathers and fuss!
Mummery! – flummery! – wusser and wuss!
All o' Humanity – Vanity Fair! –
Heaven for nothin', and – nobody there!

J. W. RILEY

A Play on Words

Assert ten barren love day made
    Dan woo'd her hart buy nigh tan day;
But when knee begged she'd marry hymn,
    The crewel bell may dancer neigh.
Lo atter fee tin vein he side
    Ant holder office offal pane –
A lasses mown touched knot terse sole –
    His grown was sever awl Lynn vane.

'Owe, beam my bride, my deer, rye prey,
    And here mice size beef ore rye dye;
Oak caste mean knot tin scorn neigh way-
    Yew are the apple love me nigh!'
She herd Dan new we truly spoke,
    Key was of noble berth, and bread
Tool lofty mean and hie renown,
    The air too great testates, 't was head.

'Ewe wood due better, sir,' she bald,
    'Took court sum mother girl, lie wean –
Ewer knot mice stile, lisle never share
    The thrown domestic azure quean!'
''Tis dun, no fare butt Scilly won –
    Aisle waist know father size on the!'
Oft tooth the nay bring porte tea flue
    And through himself into the see.

EUGENE FIELD

An Original Love-Story

He struggled to kiss her. She struggled the same
    To prevent him so bold and undaunted;
But, as smitten by lightning, he heard her exclaim,
    'Avaunt, Sir!' and off he avaunted.

But when he returned, with the fiendishest laugh,
　Showing clearly that he was affronted,
And threatened by main force to carry her off,
　She cried 'Don't!' and the poor fellow donted.

When he meekly approached, and sat down at her feet,
　Praying aloud, as before he had ranted,
That she would forgive him and try to be sweet,
　And said 'Can't you!' the dear girl recanted.

Then softly he whispered, 'How could you do so?
　I certainly thought I was jilted;
But come thou with me, to the parson we'll go;
　Say, wilt thou, my dear?' and she wilted.

                                        ANON.

The Bus

　　You cannot cuss
　　The motor bus
　　And brilliant wit
　　Is lost on it.

W. J. TURNER (HENRY AIRBUBBLE)

A Henley Barcarolle

BY A PARASYLLABIC SWAIN

My Lovylade, I peg and bray
That you will pun my joint today;
And we will, dreaming o'er the stodge,
In some remote lackwater bodge.

We'll take a man JOE, bandoline,
And hick-cup, as we slop between
The bangled tanks – we'll sink and drip,
And strum the things on board our ship.

List to my lovesick mew, and come
Far from the giddy, higgling gum!
Relaying hearses, we will croon,
And through each glowering hide we'll *spoon!*

ARTHUR A. SYKES

An Inge-nious Rhyme on the Gloomy Dean

If you his temper would unhinge
And his most sacred rights infringe
Or, excommunicated, singe
Where fiends forever writhe and cringe
Imploring that a drop of ginge-
Rale may on their tongues impinge,
　Address him then as Doctor Inge;
But if you prize the proper thing
Be sure you call him Doctor Ing,
(Unless, your ignorance to screen,
You temporize with Mister Dean),
But be advised by me and cling
To the example of the King
　And fearlessly pronounce him Ing.
Then rush to hear him have his fling
In Paul's and places where they sing.

BERNARD SHAW

Who'll Buy my Lingual?

OR

YOU PRONOUNCE PLUIE, LOUIE

I wander through a Paris shower,
Off to inspect a flat *à louer*.

The water pours as from a pitcher
On walls inscribed *Défense d'afficher*,

If I have splashed through such a pond,
I don't remember *où* or *quand*.

With raindrops glistening on my garment,
I reach my goal I don't know *comment*.

I ring, I do not wish to trespass,
For trespassing is naughty, *n'est-ce pas?*

The stairway irks my fallen arch,
Because one learns *l'ascenseur ne marche*.

I like the flat; with cheerful mien
I murmur to the man, '*Combien?*'

He mentions his idea of payment,
I say that it's exorbitant, *vraiment* –

Have I misunderstood his statement?
I do not speak the French *parfaitement*.

He mentions a reduced emolument,
I cry that it's a deal, *absolument*.

And now I think a glass of wine
Would not be too unpleasant, *hein?*

OGDEN NASH

Chacun À Son Berlitz

French is easy.
At speaking French I am the champ of the Champs-Élysée,
And since I can speak Parisian without a flaw,
I will tell you why the crows, or les corbeaux, always win their
       battle against the scarecrows: it's on account of their
       esprit de caw.

OGDEN NASH

Oddly

Oddly is a quiet land
With simple things on every hand,
With hair-lines over beetling brows
And udders under milking cows
And like as not a lonely mouse
In every single double house.

In such a land I love to be
And watch the days come up to me,
And spend the afternoons in play,
And mornings go to work and spray
With arsenic the beetling brows,
And delactate the milking cows,
And set out cheese for lonely mice
Who think the cheese I make is nice.

CLARK STILLMAN

Nomenclaturik

There was a young fellow named Cholmondeley,
Whose bride was so mellow and colmondeley
That the best man, Colquhoun,
An inane young bolqufoun,
Could only stand still and stare dolmondeley.

The bridegroom's first cousin, young Belvoir,
Whose dad was a Lancashire welvoir,
Arrived with George Bohun
At just about nohun
When excitement was mounting to felvoir.

The vicar – his surname was Beauchamp –
Of marriage endeavoured to teauchamp,
While the bridesmaid, Miss Marjoribanks,
Played one or two harjoripranks;
But the shoe that she threw failed to reauchamp.

HARRY HEARSON

Huntingdonshire

If anyone asked me what there is about Hunts.,
I should have to proclaim myself a dunts.
The name itself is practically useless for rhyming; I don't dispute
That there are punts, stunts, shunts, and even Lunts, but how to
    drag them in is a point which is moot.

It isn't a garden of England like Kent, nor does it foucester
Young ladies of the type found in Gloucester;
Nobody writes songs about Hunts-by-the-sea, I fear,
Nor about Hunts., Glorious Hunts., or that they come up from
    Huntingdonshire.
Yorkshire, now, has a pudding, and bred the sisters Brontë;
And is the largest English conté;
That's what I call hot stuff,
Unlike that Oliver Cromwell and quads-at-St Neots stuff.
What Hunts. needs, beyond all doubt, is some chap
To put it on the map.

D. R. PEDDY

Rhyme for Remembering How Many Nights there are in the Month

> Thirty-*one* nights hath December
> Plus six others we remember –
> Jan., July, Aug., May, Mar., Oct.
> The rest to thirty nights are docked,
> Save Feb., which twenty-nine hath clear
> And twenty-eight each un-leap year.

JUSTIN RICHARDSON

Rhyme for Remembering the Date of Easter

No need for confusion if we but recall
That Easter on the first Sunday after the full moon
    following the vernal equinox doth fall.

JUSTIN RICHARDSON

Spring in New York

Der spring is sprung,
Der grass is riz,
I wonder where dem boidies is?

Der little boids is on der wing,
Ain't dat absoid?
Der little wings is on der boid!

ANON.

Grace for a Cannibal Feast

Totem, votem very good showtem;
C. of E. religion not
Much cop!
Fine fine dish on – boss from mission!
Plenty lousy preacher but
Good chop!

D. R. PEDDY

I asked the maid in dulcet tone
To order me a buttered scone.
The silly girl has been and gone
And ordered me a buttered scone.

ANON.

Poor Emmy

There was love in his phyzzog and fish in his eye
When Nebuchadnezzar met Emily Bligh.
And Emily Bligh was so tender, and young,
With her lips so unkissed, and her song so unsung,

That the faintest come-hither from Nebuchadnezzar
Was more than was needed to get 'em togezzer.
So Nebuchadnezzar approached from the front,
Was hail-fellow-well-met, condescending and blunt
And, demanding to see all that Emmy could show,
Very near bowled her over at very first blow,
And *would* have, indeed, at his mere coming nigh,
If she could have got over that fish in his eye.
But no loving, nor hoping, no prayer, not a wish
Could obliterate phyzzog and eye, with its fish.

EDMOND KAPP

What's the Plural?

No one for spelling at a loss is
Who boldly spells Rhinocerosses;
I've known a few (I can't say lots)
Who called the beast Rhinocerots,
Though they are not so bad (O fie!)
As those who say Rhinoceri.
One I have heard (O holy Moses!)
Who plainly said Rhinoceroses,
While possibly a Fourth-Form Boy
Might venture on Rhinoceroi –
The moral that I draw from these is
The plural's what one damn well pleases.

ANON.

A 'Twiner'

What a curious sculptor is Moore!
What a very odd painter, Picasso!
What is granite with holes in it *for?*
What's the purpose of painting a lass so
    She's green and two-faced?
    Can it keep her more chaste?
    Is a twenty-foot lollabout
    Moll to your taste?
Or a butchered deformity? No, Mr Moore!
Good day to you, Pablo Picasso!

J. A. LINDON

Ghazul *

O, once I loved a young gazelle;
    for her I wrote my first ghazul.
What ghazul is, I cannot tell.
    They never told me at my school.

The young gazelle was called Ghiselle.
    The Ghazi who the land did rule
owned this gazelle. My song went well:
    Ghiselle's, Ghazi's Gazelle's Ghazul.

ALUN LLEWELLYN

Advice

Only a hock-bottle
    can hope to bottle hock,
for the taper-topped hock-bottle
has an epiglottal throttle
    made *ad hoc.*

    * Persian love-song.

As the anxious Hottentot 'll
seek his erring axolotl;
as puncture follows pot-hole
　　or as *tick* depends on *tock*,
so the hock is *propter* bottle
　　and the bottle is *post hoc*.
Then hock not your old hock-bottle
　　for it 's what 'll
　　　　bottle
　　　　hock.

ALUN LLEWELLYN

Sink Song

Scouring out the porridge pot,
　　Round and round and round!

Out with all the scraith and scoopery,
Lift the eely ooly droopery,
Chase the glubbery slubbery gloopery
　　Round and round and round!

Out with all the doleful dithery,
Ladle out the slimy slithery,
Hunt and catch the hithery thithery,
　　Round and round and round!

Out with all the obbly gubbly,
On the stove it burns so bubbly,
Use the spoon and use it doubly,
　　Round and round and round!

J. A. LINDON

WHO'D BE A POET?

∽

Plum's Dying Speech

from TWO GENTLEMEN OF SOHO

Now popes and persons, majesties and powers,
Dominions, sunsets, Kings, and macaroons,
Violets, marigolds, and moonlight falling
Like children's kisses on the mountain top.
Dukes, ferns, and shellfish, and all gentle things
In the high argument of love suspended,
Firelight at evening and the dawn of day,
Redwings and walnuts, oak, mahogany,
Lancaster, York, great Salisbury and Monmouth,
Hereford, Leicester, Northumberland, and Kent,
King's Cross, St Pancras, Euston, Waterloo –
All noble-sounding and capacious words,
Come and be mourners at my funeral,
For I am in the vestibule of death.

(Stabs self)

This is the gate and portal of my ending,
I think there doth not any word remain,
But silence and still quiet touch my lips
With the mute harmony of things unspoken.
I never was of that loud company
Which seek their harvest in a waste of words;
'*Do*' was my dictionary. And my sword
Leaped from the sheath ere I could mention it.

*(Stabs self.
He falls – then sits up again perkily)*

As you may see in some great orchestra
A little lonely fellow at the end
Sits by the cymbals, and the instruments
Thunder around him their tempestuous din, –

Flutes, horns, and oboes, harp and clarinet,
And the wild fiddles like the forest swaying
On Swedish mountains when the storm is high. –
But he, that could with one most royal clash
Startle the city and make all that music
Like the small twittering of birds appear,
Sits with his brasses, but doth make no sound
Till the conductor shall command him so.

(*Orchestra music stops*)

And leaves his cymbals and goes home at last,
Still with no sound, nor kindly thanks, nor notice,
For the conductor hath forgotten him –
So sit I here and die without a word.

(*Stabs himself and falls back on the floor*)

A. P. HERBERT

Murie Sing

Plumber is icumen in;
Bludie big tu-du.
Bloweth lampe, and showeth dampe,
And dripth the wud thru.
Bludie hel, boo-hoo!

Thawth drain, and runneth bath;
Saw sawth, and scruth scru;
Bull-kuk squirteth, leakë spurteth;
Wurry springeth up anew,
Boo-hoo, boo-hoo.

Tom Pugh, Tom Pugh, well plumbës thu, Tom Pugh;
Better job I naver nu.
Therefore will I cease boo-hoo,
Woorie not, but cry pooh-pooh,
Murie sing pooh-pooh, pooh-pooh,
Pooh-pooh!

A. Y. CAMPBELL

The Merchant of Venice

A LEGEND OF ITALY

I believe there are few
    But have heard of a Jew,
Named Shylock, of Venice, as arrant a 'screw
In money transactions as ever you knew;
An exorbitant miser, who never yet lent
A ducat at less than three hundred per cent,
Insomuch that the veriest spendthrift in Venice,
Who'd take no more care of his pounds than his pennies,
When press'd for a loan, at the very first sight
Of his terms, would back out, and take refuge in *Flight*.
It is not my purpose to pause and inquire
If he might not, in managing thus to retire
Jump out of the frying-pan into the fire;
Suffice it, that folks would have nothing to do,
Who could possibly help it, with Shylock the Jew.

But, however discreetly one cuts and contrives,
We've been most of us taught, in the course of our lives,
That 'Needs must when the Elderly Gentleman drives!'
    In proof of this rule,
    A thoughtless young fool,
Bassanio, a Lord of the Tom-noddy school,

Who, by showing at Operas, Balls, Plays, and Court,
A 'swelling' (Payne Collier would read 'swilling') 'port,
And inviting his friends to dine, breakfast, and sup,
Had shrunk his 'weak means,' and was 'stump'd' and 'hard up,'
    Took occasion to send
    To his very good friend
Antonio, a merchant whose wealth had no end
And who'd often before had the kindness to lend
Him large sums, on his note, which he'd managed to spend.

    'Antonio,' said he,
    'Now listen to me;
I've just hit on a scheme which, I think, you'll agree,
All matters consider'd, is no bad design,
And which, if it succeeds, will suit your book and mine.

'In the first place, you know all the money I've got,
Time and often, from you has been long gone to pot,
And in making those loans you have made a bad shot;

Now do as the boys do when, shooting at sparrows
And tom-tits, they chance to lose one of their arrows,
– Shoot another the same way – I'll watch well its track,
And, turtle to tripe, I'll bring both of them back! –
    So list to my plan,
    And do what you can
To attend to and second it, that's a good man!

'There's a Lady, young, handsome beyond all compare, at
A place they call Belmont, whom, when I was there, at
The suppers and parties my friend Lord Mountferrat
Was giving last season, we all used to stare at.
Then, as to her wealth, her Solicitor told mine,
Besides vast estates, a pearl-fishery, and gold mine,
    Her iron strong box
    Seems bursting its locks,

It's stuffed so with shares in "Grand Junctions" and "Docks,
Not to speak of the money she's got in the Stocks,
    French, Dutch, and Brazilian,
    Columbian, and Chilian,
In English Exchequer-bills full half a million,
Not "kites", manufactured to cheat and inveigle,
But the right sort of "flimsy," all sign'd by Monteagle.
Then I know not how much in Canal-shares and Railways,
And more speculations I need not detail, ways
Of vesting which, if not so safe as some think 'em,
Contribute a deal to improving one's income;
    In short, she's a Mint!
    – Now I say, deuce is in't
If, with all my experience, I can't take a hint,
And her "eye's speechless messages," plainer than print
At the time that I told you of, know from a squint.
    In short, my dear Tony,
    My trusty old crony,
Do stump up three thousand once more as a loan – I
Am sure of my game – though, of course, there are brutes,
Of all sorts and sizes, preferring their suits
To her, you may call the Italian Miss Coutts.
Yet Portia – she's named from that daughter of Cato's –
Is not to be snapp'd up like little potatoes,
    And I have not a doubt
    I shall rout every lout
Ere you'll whisper Jack Robinson – cut them all out –
    Surmount every barrier,
    Carry her, marry her!
– Then hey! my old Tony, when once fairly noosed,
For her Three-and-a-half per Cents – New and Reduced!'

    With a wink of his eye
    His friend made reply
In his jocular manner, sly, caustic, and dry:
'Still the same boy, Bassanio – never say "die"!

– Well – I hardly know how I shall do't, but I'll try, –
Don't suppose my affairs are at all in a hash,
But the fact is, at present I'm quite out of cash;
The bulk of my property, merged in rich cargoes, is
Tossing about, as you know, in my Argosies,
Tending, of course, my resources to cripple, – I
've one bound to England, – another to Tripoli –
Cyprus – Masulipatam – and Bombay; –
   A sixth, by the way,
   I consigned t'other day
To Sir Gregor M'Gregor, Cacique of Poyais,
A country where silver's as common as clay.
   Meantime, till they tack,
   And come, some of them, back,
What with Custom-house duties, and bills falling due,
My account with Jones Loyd, and Co., looks rather blue;
While, as for the "ready", I'm like a Church-mouse, –
I really don't think there's five pounds in the house.
   But, no matter for that,
   Let me just get my hat,
And my new silk umbrella that stands on the mat,
And we'll go forth at once to the market – we two, –
And try what my credit in Venice can do;
I stand well on 'Change, and, when all's said and done, I
Don't doubt I shall get it for love or for money.'

   They were going to go,
   When, lo! down below,
In the street, they heard somebody crying, 'Old Clo'!
– 'By the Pope, there's the man for our purpose! – I knew
We should not have to search long. Solanio, run you,
– Salarino, – quick! – haste! ere he get out of view,
And call in that scoundrel, old Shylock the Jew!'

With a pack,
Like a sack
Of old clothes at his back,
And three hats on his head, Shylock came in a crack,
Saying, 'Rest you fair, Signior Antonio! – vat, pray,
Might your vorship be pleashed for to vant in ma vay?'

– 'Why, Shylock, although,
As you very well know,
I am what they call "warm", – pay my way as I go,
And, as to myself, neither borrow nor lend,
I can break through a rule to oblige an old friend;
And that's the case now – Lord Bassanio would raise
Some three thousand ducats – well, – knowing your ways,
And that nought's to be got from you, say what one will,
Unless you've a couple of names to the bill,
Why, for once, I'll put mine to it,
Yea, seal and sign to it –
Now, then, old Sinner, let's hear what you'll say
As to "doing" a bill at three months from today?
Three thousand gold ducats, mind – all in good bags
Of hard money – no sealing-wax, slippers, or rags!'

' – Vell, ma tear,' says the Jew,
'I'll see vat I can do!
But Mishter Antonio, hark you, tish funny
You say to me, "Shylock, ma tear, ve'd have money!"
Ven you very vell knows
How you shpit on ma clothes,
And use naughty vords – call me Dog – and avouch
Dat I put too much int'resht py half in ma pouch,
And vhile I, like de resht of ma tribe, shrug and crouch,
You find fault mit ma pargains, and say I'm a Smouch.
– Vell! – no matters, ma tear, –
Von vord in your ear!
I'd be friends mit you bote – and to make dat appear,

Vy, I'll find you de monies as soon as you vill,
Only von littel joke musht be put in de pill; –
   Ma tear, you musht say,
   If on such and such day
Such sum or such sums, you shall fail to repay,
I shall cut vhere I like, as de pargain is proke,
A fair pound of your flesh – chest by vay of a joke.'

   So novel a clause
   Caused Bassanio to pause;
But Antonio, like most of those sage 'Johnny Raws'
   Who care not three straws
   About Lawyers or Laws,
And think cheaply of 'Old Father Antic', because
They have never experienced a gripe from his claws,
'Pooh pooh'd' the whole thing. – 'Let the Smouch have his way –
   Why, what care I, pray,
   For his penalty? – Nay,
It's a forfeit he'd never expect me to pay;
   And, come what come may,
   I hardly need say
My ships will be back a full month ere the day.'
So, anxious to see his friend off on his journey,
And thinking the whole but a paltry concern, he
   Affix'd with all speed
   His name to a deed,
Duly stamp'd and drawn up by a sharp Jew attorney.
Thus again furnish'd forth, Lord Bassanio, instead
Of squandering the cash, after giving one spread,
With fiddling and masques, at the Saracen's Head,
   In the morning 'made play',
   And without more delay,
Started off in the steam-boat for Belmont next day.
   But scarcely had he
   From the harbour got free,
And left the Lagunes for the broad open sea,

Ere the 'Change and Rialto both rung with the news
That he'd carried off more than mere cash from the Jew's.

Though Shylock was old,
And, if rolling in gold,
Was as ugly a dog as you'd wish to behold,
For few in his tribe 'mongst their Levis and Moseses
Sported so Jewish an eye, beard, and nose as his,
Still, whate'er the opinions of Horace and some be,
Your *aquilae* generate *some*times *Columbae*,
Like Jephthah, as Hamlet says, he'd 'one fair daughter',
And every gallant, who caught sight of her, thought her,
A jewel – a gem of the very first water;
A great many sought her,
Till one at last caught her,
And, upsetting all that the Rabbis had taught her,
To feelings so truly reciprocal brought her,
That the very same night
Bassanio thought right
To give all his old friends that farewell 'invite',
And while Shylock was gone there to feed out of spite,
On 'wings made by a tailor' the damsel took flight.

By these 'wings' I'd express
A grey duffle dress,
With brass badge and muffin cap, made, as by rule,
For an upper class boy in the National School.
Jessy ransack'd the house, popp'd her breeks on, and when so
Disguised, bolted off with her beau – one Lorenzo,
An 'Unthrift', who lost not a moment in whisking
Her into the boat,
And was fairly afloat
Ere her Pa had got rid of the smell of the griskin.
Next day, while old Shylock was making a racket,
And threatening how well he'd dust every man's jacket
Who'd help'd her in getting aboard of the packet,

Bassanio at Belmont was capering and prancing,
And bowing, and scraping, and singing, and dancing,
Making eyes at Miss Portia, and doing his best
To perform the polite, and to cut out the rest;
And, if left to herself, he no doubt had succeeded,
For none of them waltz'd so genteelly as he did;
   But an obstacle lay,
   Of some weight, in his way,
The defunct Mr P. who was now turned to clay,
Had been an odd man, and, though all for the best he meant,
Left but a queer sort of 'Last will and testament' –
   Bequeathing her hand,
   With her houses and land,
&c., from motives one don't understand,
As she rev'renced his memory, and valued his blessing,
To him who should turn out the best hand at guessing!

   Like a good girl, she did
   Just what she was bid;
In one of three caskets her picture she hid,
And clapp'd a conundrum a-top of each lid.

A couple of Princes, a black and a white one,
Tried first, but they both fail'd in choosing the right one.
Another from Naples, who shoe'd his own horses;
A French Lord, whose graces might vie with Count D'Orsay's; –
A young English Baron; – a Scotch Peer his neighbour:-
A dull drunken Saxon, all moustache and sabre; –
All follow'd, and all had their pains for their labour.
Bassanio came last – happy man be his dole!
Put his conjuring cap on, – consider'd the whole, –
   The gold put aside as
   Mere 'hard food for Midas',
   The silver bade trudge
   As a 'pale common drudge';
Then choosing the little lead box in the middle,
Came plump on the picture, and found out the riddle.

Now you're not such a goose as to think, I dare say,
Gentle Reader, that all this was done in a day,
    Any more than the dome
    Of St Peter's at Rome
Was built in the same space of time; and, in fact,
    Whilst Bassanio was doing
    His billing and cooing,
Three months had gone by ere he reach'd the fifth act,
Meanwhile that unfortunate bill became due,
Which his Lordship had almost forgot, to the Jew,
    And Antonio grew
    In a deuce of a stew,
For he could not cash up, spite of all he could do;
(The bitter old Israelite would not renew),
What with contrary winds, storms, and wrecks, and embargoes, his
Funds were all stopp'd, or gone down in his argosies,
None of the set having come into port,
And Shylock's attorney was moving the Court
For the forfeit supposed to be set down in sport.

    The serious news,
    Of this step of the Jew's,
And his fix'd resolution all terms to refuse,
Gave the newly-made Bridegroom a fit of 'the Blues',
Especially, too, as it came from the pen
Of his poor friend himself on the wedding-day, – then,
When the Parson had scarce shut his book up, and when
The Clerk was yet uttering the final Amen.

'Dear Friend,' it continued, 'all's up with me – I
Have nothing on earth now to do but to die!
And, as death clears all scores, you're no longer my debtor;
    I should take it as kind
    Could you come – never mind –
If your love don't persuade you, why, – don't let this letter!'

I hardly need say this was scarcely read o'er
   Ere a post-chaise and four
   Was brought round to the door,
And Bassanio, though, doubtless, he thought it a bore,
Gave his Lady one kiss, and then started at score.
   But scarce in his flight
   Had he got out of sight
Ere Portia, addressing a groom, said, 'My lad, you a
Journey must take on the instant to Padua;
Find out there Bellario, a Doctor of Laws,
Who, like Follett, is never left out of a cause,
   And give him this note,
   Which I've hastily wrote,
Take the papers he'll give you – then push for the ferry
Below, where I'll meet you, you'll do't in a wherry,
If you can't find a boat on the Brenta with sails to it –
– Stay, bring his gown too, and wig with three tails to it.'

   Giovanni (that's Jack)
   Brought out his hack,
Made a bow to his mistress, then jump'd on its back,
Put his hand to his hat, and was off in a crack.
The Signora soon follow'd, herself, taking, as her
Own escort Nerissa, her maid, and Balthasar.

        *

'The Court is prepared, the Lawyers are met,
The Judges all ranged, a terrible show!'
As Captain Macheath says, – and when one's in debt,
The sight's as unpleasant a one as I know,
Yet still not so bad after all, I suppose,
As if, when one cannot discharge what one owes,
They should bid people cut off one's toes or one's nose;
   Yet here, a worse fate,
   Stands Antonio, of late
A Merchant, might vie e'en with Princes in state.

With his waistcoat unbutton'd, prepared for the knife,
Which, in taking a pound of flesh, must take his life;
– On the other side Shylock, his bag on the floor,
And three shocking bad hats on his head, as before,
    Imperturbable stands,
    As he waits their commands
With his scales and great *snicker-snee* in his hands:
– Between them, equipt in a wig, gown, and bands,
With a very smooth face, a young dandified Lawyer,
Whose air, ne'ertheless, speaks him quite a top-sawyer,
    Though his hopes are but feeble,
    Does his *possible*
To make the hard Hebrew to mercy incline,
And in lieu of his three thousand ducats take nine,
Which Bassanio, for reasons we well may divine,
Shows in so many bags all drawn up in a line.
But vain are all efforts to soften him – still
    He points to the bond
    He so often has conn'd,
And says in plain terms he'll be shot if he will.
So the dandified Lawyer, with talking grown hoarse,
Says, 'I *can* say no more – let the law take its course.'

Just fancy the gleam of the eye of the Jew,
As he sharpen'd his knife on the sole of his shoe
    From the toe to the heel,
    And grasping the steel,
With a business-like air was beginning to feel
Whereabouts he should cut, as a butcher would veal,
When the dandified Judge puts a spoke in his wheel.
    'Stay, Shylock,' says he,
    'Here's one thing – you see
This bond of yours gives you here no jot of blood!
– The words are "A pound of flesh", – that's clear as mud –
Slice away, then, old fellow – but mind! – if you spill
One drop of his claret that's not in your bill,

I'll hang you, like Haman! – by Jingo I will!
   When apprised of this flaw,
   You never yet saw
Such an awfully mark'd elongation of jaw
As in Shylock, who cried, 'Plesh ma heart! ish dat law?' –
   Off went his three hats,
   And he look'd as the cats
Do, whenever a mouse has escaped from their claw.
' – Ish't the law?' – why the thing won't admit of a query –
   'No doubt of the fact,
   Only look at the act;
Acto quinto, cap: tertio, Dogi Falieri –
Nay, if, rather than cut you'd relinquish the debt,
The Law, Master Shy, has a hold on you yet.
See Foscari's "Statutes at large" – "If a Stranger
A Citizen's life shall, with malice, endanger,
The whole of his property, little or great,
Shall go, on conviction, one half to the State,
And one to the person pursued by his hate;
   And, not to create
   Any further debate,
The Doge, if he pleases, may cut off his pate."
So down on your marrowbones, Jew, and ask mercy!
Defendant and Plaintiff are now *wisy wersy*.'

   What need to declare
   How pleased they all were
At so joyful an end to so sad an affair?
Or Bassanio's delight at the turn things had taken,
His friend having saved, to the letter, his bacon? –
How Shylock got shaved, and turn'd Christian, though late.
To save a life-int'rest in half his estate? –
How the dandified Lawyer, who'd managed the thing,
Would not take any fee for his pains but a ring
Which Mrs Bassanio had giv'n her spouse,
With injunctions to keep it, on leaving the house? –

How when he, and the spark
    Who appeared as his clerk,
Had thrown off their wigs, and their gowns, and their jetty coats
There stood Nerissa and Portia in petticoats? –
How they pouted, and flouted, and acted the cruel,
Because Lord Bassanio had not kept his jewel? –
    How they scolded and broke out,
    Till, having their joke out,
They kissed, and were friends, and, all blessing and blessed,
    Drove home by the light
    Of a moonshiny night,
Like the one in which Troilus, the brave Trojan knight,
Sat astride on a wall, and sigh'd after his Cressid? –

    All this, if 'twere meet,
    I'd go on to repeat,
But a story spun out so's by no means a treat,
So, I'll merely relate what, in spite of the pains
I have taken to rummage among his remains,
No edition of Shakespeare, I've met with, contains;
But, if the account which I've heard be the true one,
We shall have it, no doubt, before long, in a new one.

    In an M S, then, sold
    For its full weight in gold,
And knock'd down to my friend, Lord Tomnoddy, I'm told
It's recorded that Jessy, coquettish and vain,
Gave her husband, Lorenzo, a good deal of pain;
Being mildly rebuked, she levanted again,
Ran away with a Scotchman, and, crossing the main,
Became known by the name of the 'Flower of Dumblane'.

That Antonio, whose piety caused, as we've seen,
Him to spit upon every old Jew's gaberdine,
    And whose goodness to paint
    All colours were faint,
Acquired the well-merited prefix of 'Saint',

And the Doge, his admirer, of honour the fount,
Having given him a patent, and made him a Count,
He went over to England, got nat'raliz'd there,
And espous'd a rich heiress in Hanover Square.

That Shylock came with him, no longer a Jew,
But converted, I think may be possibly true,
But that Walpole, as these self-same papers aver,
By changing the *y* in his name into *er*,
Should allow him a fictitious surname to dish up,
And in Seventeen-twenty-eight make him a Bishop,
I cannot believe – but shall still think them two men
Till some Sage proves the fact 'with his usual *acumen*'.

MORAL

From this tale of the Bard
It's uncommonly hard
If an editor can't draw a moral. – 'Tis clear,
Then, – In ev'ry young wife-seeking Bachelor's ear
A maxim, 'bove all other stories, this one drums,
'PITCH GREEK TO OLD HARRY, AND STICK TO CONUNDRUMS!!

To new-married Ladies this lesson it teaches,
'You're "no that far wrong" in assuming the breeches!'

Monied men upon 'Change, and rich Merchants it schools
To look well to assets – nor play with edge tools!
Last of all, this remarkable History shows men,
What caution they need when they deal with old-clothesmen!
So bid John and Mary
To mind and be wary,
And never let one of them come down the are'!

R. H. BARHAM

Sonnet CII

TO A PACKET OF TWENTY

Farewell, thou art too dear for my possessing,
Now will I buy thee at so vain expense;
The vile increase, my slender hope decreasing,
Sets thee and me at hateful difference.
For how shall I, without access of plenty,
At thy fond value waste my lowly store,
Or give in fee for thine encarded twenty
Out of my hungry purse a farthing more?
Thyself thou gav'st, in smoke my substance burning,
And I, thy prodigal, too idly willing,
Who, bankrupt now, thy sweet persuasion spurning,
Forswear thy love to save mine extra shilling:
    Thus shall I lose thee, though in wealth a winner,
    Perforce a saint, yet still in heart a sinner.

G. H. VALLINS

From 'Chrononhotonthologos'

THE MOST TRAGICAL TRAGEDY

KING: Hashéd pork! shall Chrononhotonthologos
    Be fed with swine's flesh, and at second hand?
    Now, by the gods! thou dost insult us, general!
BOMBARDINION:
    The gods can witness that I little thought
    Your Majesty to other flesh than this
    Had aught the least propensity. [*Points to the ladies.*]
KING: Is this a dinner for a hungry monarch?
BOMB: Monarchs, as great as Chrononhotonthologos,
    Have made a very hearty meal of worse.

KING : Ha! traitor! dost thou brave me to my teeth?
　　　　Take this reward, and learn to mock thy master. [*Strikes him.*]
BOMB : A blow! shall Bombardinion take a blow?
　　　　Blush! blush, thou sun! start back, thou rapid ocean!
　　　　Hills! vales! seas! mountains! all commixing crumble,
　　　　And into chaos pulverize the world;
　　　　For Bombardinion has received a blow,
　　　　And Chrononhotonthologos shall die. [*Draws.*]

　　　　[*The women run off, crying, 'Help! Murder!' etc.*]

KING : What means the traitor?
BOMB : 　　　　　　　　　Traitor in thy teeth,
　　　　Thus I defy thee!

　　　　　[*They fight, he kills the King.*]

　　　　　　　　Ha! what have I done?
　　　　Go, call a coach, and let a coach be called;
　　　　And let the man that calls it be the caller;
　　　　And, in his calling, let him nothing call,
　　　　But coach! coach! coach! Oh! for a coach, ye gods.

　　　　　[*Exit raving. Returns with a* DOCTOR.]

BOMB : How fares your Majesty?
DOCT : My lord, he's dead.
BOMB : Ha! dead! impossible! it cannot be!
　　　　I'd not believe it tho' himself should swear it,
　　　　Go join his body to his soul again,
　　　　Or, by this light, thy soul shall quit thy body.
DOCT : My lord, he's far beyond the power of physic,
　　　　His soul has left his body and this world.
BOMB : Then go t'other world and fetch it back. [*Kills him.*]

　　　　　　　　　　　　　　　HENRY CAREY

Mr Smith Tries in vain to Telephone

Soe hee
His eager Steps pursu'd, with Purpose clere
And unfulfill'd Intent, nor turn'd, nor stay'd
His onward Course, impatient to inspire
With urgent Speech the Engin sensible
To Breath articulate. Yet al in vaine:
Him of his swift Converse unequall Fate
Bereft, and in the silent solitary Street
Left impotent. His angry Eyes aflame
Like living Coales the glassy Tower transfix'd,
Where unrepentant, careless, unashamed,
A son of *Belial* to the ekkoing Wire
Outpour'd his foolish love, with sweet Delay
Entranc'd, al els forgot. He long in Hope
Kept faithfull watch, though vaine; as once of old
The hapless Mother from her Casement gaz'd
Al unavailing, for his glad Return
Whom in her Tent the avenging *Kenite* pierc'd
With sharp and bitter Nail; or *Ceres* fair
Awaited long her deare *Persephone*
By *Pluto's* guile ensnar'd. In deep Despaire,
And by Frustration rack'd, at last he turn'd
Unsatisfied away; what time the Other, stirr'd
By garrulous Emotion, straight renew'd
Interminable Speech and soft Discourse
Unending. ...

G. H. VALLINS

The Curate to his Slippers

Take, oh take those boots away,
    That so nearly are outworn;
And those shoes remove, I pray –
    Pumps that but induce the corn!
But my slippers bring again,
        Bring again;
Works of love, but worked in vain,
        Worked in vain!

                    HORATIO SMITH

At the Cock Tavern

Champagne doth not a Luncheon make
    Nor caviare a meal;
Men gluttonous and rich may take
    These till they make them ill.
If I've potatoes to my chop,
    And after that have cheese,
Angels in Pond and Spiers's shop
    Serve no such luxuries.

                    HORATIO SMITH

Election Anacreontic

Gather ye bank-notes while ye may;
    The happy time is flitting;
The Member canvassing today
    Tomorrow will be sitting.

That glorious crib, the *Rising Sun*,
    Where patriots are glowing,
Too soon its brilliant course is run,
    Its beer will soon stop flowing.

ANON.

Evening

AN ELEGY BY A POETICAL CARMAN

Apollo now, Sol's carman, drives his stud
    Home to the mews that's seated in the West,
And custom's clerks, like him, through Thames Street mud,
    Now westering wind, in Holland trousers dressed.

So from the stands the empty carts are dragged,
    The horses homeward to their stable go,
And mine, with hauling heavy hogsheads fagged,
    Prepare to take the luxury of – 'Wo!'

Now from the slaughter-houses cattle roar,
    Knowing that with the morn their lives they yields,
And Mr Sweetman's gig is at the door
    To take him to his house in Hackney Fields.

Closed are the gates of the West India Docks,
    Rums, Sugars, Coffees, find at length repose,
And I, with other careless carmen, flocks
    To the King's Head, the Chequers, or the Rose.

They smoke a pipe – the shepherd's pipe I wakes,
    Them skittles pleases – me the Muse invites,
They in their ignorance to drinking takes,
    I, blessed with learning, takes a pen and writes.

HORACE SMITH

The Owl's Reply to Gray

Who, who has dared to treat us owls so ill ?
(With us, of course it's U to use two whos)
To whomsoe'er it was, I take my quill
To twit him for his quite erroneous views.

Doubtless some elegiac poet grey,
Too witless and too wooden in the head
To understand a whit of what I say,
Has misconstrued my twilight serenade.

No, I did not complain, I'm not a grouse
(I do not give two hoots when I am blue)
You heard me call my love to share a mouse
For that's our owlish way, to wit, to woo.

F. SINCLAIR

From our Austerity Anthology

ELEGY W.I. A COUNTRY CHURCHYARD BY T. G.

The curfew t's the k. of parting day.
The village elders in the churchyard plot
Might have been famous men like (e.g.) Gray;
But famous people also die. So what?

JUSTIN RICHARDSON

The House that Jack Built

1. Behold the Mansion rear'd by daedal Jack.

2. See the Malt stor'd in many a plethoric sack
   In the proud cirque of Ivan's bivouac.

3. Mark how the Rat's felonious fangs invade
   The golden stores in John's pavilion laid.

4. Anon, with velvet foot and Tarquin strides,
   Subtle Grimalkin to his quarry glides,
   Grimalkin grim, that slew the fierce rodent
   Whose tooth, insidious, Johann's sackcloth rent.

5. Lo! now the deep-mouth'd Canine Foe's assault
   That vex'd th' avenger of the stolen malt,
   Stor'd in the hallow'd precincts of that hall
   That rose complete at Jack's creative call.

6. Here stalks th' impetuous Cow with crumpled horn,
   Whereon th' exacerbating hound was torn,
   Who bay'd the feline slaughter-beast that slew
   The rat predaceous, whose keen fangs ran through
   The textile fibres that involv'd the grain
   Which lay in Han's inviolate domain.

7. Here walks, forlorn, the Damsel crown'd with rue,
   Lactiferous spoils from vaccine dugs who drew
   Of that corniculate beast whose tortuous horn
   Tossed to the clouds, in fierce vindictive scorn,
   The harrying hound whose braggart bark and stir
   Arch'd the lithe spine and rear'd th' indignant fur
   Of puss, that with verminicidal claw
   Struck the weird rat, in whose insatiate maw
   Lay reeking malt that erst in Juan's courts we saw.

8. Rob'd in senescent garb, that seems, in sooth,
   Too long a prey to Chronos' iron tooth,
   Behold the Man whose amorous lips incline,
   Full with young Eros' osculative sign,
   To the lorn maiden whose lactalbic hands
   Drew albulactic wealth from lacteal glands
   Of that immortal bovine by whose horn
   Distort to realms ethereal was borne

The beast Catulean, vexer of that sly
Ulysses quadrupedal who made die
The old mordaceous rat that dared devour
Antecedaneous ale in John's domestic bower.

9. Lo here! with hirsute honours doff'd, succinct
Of saponaceous locks, the Priest who link'd
In Hymen's golden bands the torn unthrift
Whose means exiguous star'd from many a rift,
Even as he kiss'd the virgin all forlorn.
Who milk'd the cow with implicated horn,
Who in fine wrath the canine torturer skied
That dar'd to vex th' insidious muricide
Who let auroral effluence through the pelt
Of the sly rat that robb'd the place Jack built.

10. The loud cantankerous Shangae comes at last,
Whose shouts arouse the shorn ecclesiast
Who seal'd the vows of Hymen's sacrament
To him who, rob'd in garments indigent,
Inosculates the damsel lachrymose,
Th' emulgator of that horn'd brute morose
That tossed the dog that worried the cat that kilt
The rat that ate the malt that lay i' th' house Jack built.

ANON.

Es war ein König in Thule

There was a toff in Thule,
A gallows gent and brave,
To whom 'is dying Jooley,
A nansome tankard gave.

Twas 'arf 'is soul – you twigged it –
'e prized it, pore old chap:
And ever, as 'e swigged it,
'is eyes turned on the tap.

And ere 'e kicked the bucket
Beset by kinsmen smug,
'e warned the blighters 'chuck it,
'ands off that bloody mug.

Not yet I've quit the tiller,
So axe the boys to meet,
And in my seaside viller
I'll stand the crowd a treat.'

Up stood that game old party,
(The Beano'd gone off well):
'e downed 'is tiddley 'earty,
Then 'urled the cup to 'ell.

'e saw the pot a-sinking
And rinking round the sea,
'is ole mince pies was blinking,
And never more drunk 'e.

JOHN SAMPSON

Sonnet IV of the Amatory Poems of Abel Shufflebottom

I would I were that portly gentleman
With gold-laced hat and golden-headed cane,
Who hangs in Delia's parlour! But whene'er
From books or needlework her looks arise,
On him CONVERGE THE SUNBEAMS OF HER EYES
And he UNBLAMED may gaze upon MY FAIR,
And oft MY FAIR his FAVOUR'D form surveys.
O HAPPY PICTURE! still on HER to gaze;
I envy him! and jealous fear alarms,
Lest the STRONG *glance* of those *divinest* charms
WARM HIM TO LIFE, as in the ancient days,
When MARBLE MELTED in Pygmalion's arms.
I would I were that portly gentleman
With gold-laced hat and golden-headed cane.

ROBERT SOUTHEY

The Village Burglar

Under a spreading gooseberry bush the village burglar lies.
The burglar is a hairy man with whiskers round his eyes
And the muscles of his brawny arms keep off the little flies.

He goes on Sunday to the church to hear the Parson shout.
He puts a penny in the plate and takes a sovereign out,
And drops a conscience-stricken tear in case he is found out.

ANON.

The Course of Time

Robert Pollok, A. M.! this work of yours
Is meant, I do not doubt, extremely well,
And the design I deem most laudable,
But since I find the book laid on my table,
I shall presume (with the fair owner's leave)
To note a single slight deficiency:
I mean, in short (since it is called a poem)
That in the course of ten successive books
If something in the shape of poetry
Were to be met with, we should like it better;
But nothing of the kind is to be found,
Nothing, alas! but words of the olden time,
Quaint and uncouth, contorted phrase and queer,
With the familiar language that befits
Tea-drinking parties most unmeetly matched.

J. H. FRERE

To a Bottle of Old Port

When he who adores thee has left but the dregs
  Of such famous old Stingo behind,
Oh! say will he bluster and weep – no 'ifegs!
  He'll seek for some more of the kind.
He'll laugh and, though doctors perhaps may condemn,
  Thy tide shall efface the decree,
For many can witness, though subject to phlegm,
  He has always been faithful to thee!

With thee were the dreams of his earliest love,
  Every rap in his pocket was thine,
And his very last prayer, ev'ry morning, by Jove!
  Was to finish the evening in wine.

How blest are the tipplers whose heads can outlive
    The effects of four bottles of thee;
But the next dearest blessing that Heaven can give,
    Is to stagger home muzzy from three!

WILLIAM MAGINN

From 'The Thieves' Anthology'

I met a cracksman coming down the Strand,
    Who said, 'A huge Cathedral, piled of stone,
Stands in a churchyard, near St Martin's Le Grand,
    Where keeps St Paul his sacerdotal throne.
A street runs by it to the northward. There
For cab and bus is writ, "No Thoroughfare",
    The Mayor and Councilmen do so command,
And in that street a shop, with many a box,
    Upon whose sign these fateful words I scanned:
"My name is Chubb, who makes the Patent Locks;
    Look on my works, ye burglars, and despair!"'
Here made he pause, like one who sees a blight
    Mar all his hopes, and sighed with drooping air,
'Our game is up, my covies, blow me tight!'

THEODORE MARTIN

Inscription

For the Door of the Cell in Newgate, where Mrs Brownrigg, the
'Prentice-cide, was confined previous to her Execution.

For one long term, or e'er her trial came,
Here Brownrigg lingered. Often have these cells
Echoed her blasphemies, as with shrill voice
She screamed for fresh Geneva. Not to her
Did the blithe fields of Tothill, or thy street,

St Giles, its fair varieties expand;
Till at the last, in slow-drawn cart she went
To execution. Dost thou ask her crime?
SHE WHIPPED TWO FEMALE 'PRENTICES TO DEATH,
AND HID THEM IN THE COAL-HOLE. For her mind
Shaped strictest plans of discipline. Sage schemes!
Such as Lycurgus taught, when at the shrine
Of the Orthyan goddess he bade flog
The little Spartans; such as erst chastised
Our Milton, when at college. For this act
Did Brownrigg swing. Harsh laws! But time shall come
When France shall reign, and laws be all repealed!

GEORGE CANNING and J. H. FRERE

Striking

It was a railway passenger,
    And he lept up jauntilie.
'Now up and bear, thou stout portèr,
    My two chattèls to me.

'Bring hither, bring hither my bag so red,
    And portmanteau so brown
(They lie in the van, for a trusty man
    He labelled them London town):

'And fetch me eke a cabman bold,
    That I may be his fare, his fare;
And he shall have a good shilling.
If by two of the clock he do me bring
    To the terminus, Euston Square.'

'Now, – so to thee the saints alway
    Good gentleman, give luck, –
As never a cab may I find this day,
    For the cabmen wights have struck:

'And now, I wis, at the Red Post Inn,
    Or else at the Dog and Duck,
Or at Unicorn Blue, or at Green Griffin,
The nut-brown ale and the fine old gin
    Right pleasantly they do suck.'

'Now rede me aright, thou stout portèr,
    What were it best that I should do:
For woe is me, an' I reach not there
    Or ever the clock strike two.'

'I have a son, a lytel son;
    Fleet is his foot as the wild roebuck's:
Give him a shilling and eke a brown,
And he shall carry thy fardels down
To Euston, or half over London town,
    On one of the station trucks.'

Then forth in a hurry did they twain fare,
The gent, and the son of the stout portèr,
Who fled like an arrow, nor turned a hair,
    Through all the mire and the muck:
'A ticket, a ticket, sir clerk, I pray:
For by two of the clock must I needs away.'
'That may hardly be', the clerk did say,
    'For indeed – the clocks have struck.'

C. S. CALVERLEY

I'm a Shrimp

I'm a shrimp! I'm a shrimp, of diminutive size:
Inspect my antennae, and look at my eyes;
I'm a natural syphon, when dipped in a cup,
For I drain the contents to the very last drop up.
I care not for craw-fish, I heed not the prawn,
From a flavour especial my fame has been drawn;

Nor e'en to the crab or the lobster do yield,
When I'm properly cooked and efficiently peeled.
Quick! quick! pile the coals – let your saucepan be deep,
For the weather is warm, and I'm sure not to keep;
Off, off with my head – split my shell into three –
I'm a shrimp! I'm a shrimp – to be eaten with tea.

R. B. BROUGH

The Wife

Her washing ended with the day,
　　Yet lived she at its close.
And passed the long, long night away,
　　In darning ragged hose.

But when the sun in all his state
　　Illumed the eastern skies,
She passed about the kitchen grate
　　And went to making pies.

PHOEBE CARY

Brahma

If the wild bowler thinks he bowls,
　　Or if the batsman thinks he's bowled,
They know not, poor misguided souls,
　　They, too, shall perish unconsoled.
I am the batsman and the bat,
　　I am the bowler and the ball,
The umpire, the pavilion cat,
　　The roller, pitch, and stumps, and all.

ANDREW LANG

If thou wouldst visit fair Melrose aright,
Go visit it at pale moonlight.
If thou wouldst visit it awrong
Go visit it by charrybong.

ANON.

The Willow-Tree

Long by the willow-tree
   Vainly they sought her,
Wild rang the mother's screams
   O'er the gray water.
'Where is my lovely one?
   Where is my daughter?

'Rouse thee, sir constable –
   Rouse thee and look.
Fisherman, bring your net,
   Boatman, your hook;
Beat in the lily beds,
   Dive in the brook.'

Vainly the constable
   Shouted and called her;
Vainly the fisherman
   Beat the green alder;
Vainly he threw the net,
   Never it hauled her!

Mother beside the fire
   Sat, her night-cap in;
Father, in easy chair,
   Gloomily napping;
When at the window-sill
   Came a light tapping.

And a pale countenance
   Looked through the casement:
Loud beat the mother's heart,
   Sick with amazement,
And at the vision which
   Came to surprise her!
Shrieking in an agony –
   'Lor! it's Elizar!'

Yes, 'twas Elizabeth;
   Yes, 'twas their girl;
Pale was her cheek, and her
   Hair out of curl.
'Mother!' the loved one,
   Blushing, exclaimed,
'Let not your innocent
   Lizzy be blamed.

'Yesterday, going to Aunt
   Jones's to tea,
Mother, dear mother, I
   Forgot the door-key!
And as the night was cold,
   And the way steep,
Mrs Jones kept me to
   Breakfast and sleep.'

Whether her pa and ma
   Fully believed her,
That we shall never know;
   Stern they received her;
And for the work of that
   Cruel, though short night, –
Sent her to bed without
   Tea for a fortnight.

MORAL

Hey diddle diddlety,
    Cat and the fiddlety,
Maidens of England take
    Caution by she!
    Let love and suicide
    Never tempt you aside,
And always remember to take the door-key.

W. M. THACKERAY

Mrs Judge Kenkins

BEING THE ONLY GENUINE SEQUEL TO WHITTIER'S
'MAUD MÜLLER'

Maud Müller, all that summer day,
Raked the meadows sweet with hay;

Yet, looking down the distant lane,
She hoped the judge would come again.

And when he came, with smile and bow,
Maud only blushed, and stammered, 'Ha-ow?'

And spoke of her 'pa', and wondered whether
He'd give consent they should wed together.

Old Müller burst in tears, and then
Begged that the judge would lend him 'ten';

For trade was dull and wages low,
And the 'crops' this year were somewhat slow.

And ere the languid summer died,
Sweet Maud became the Judge's bride.

But on the day that they were mated
Maud's brother Bob was intoxicated;

And Maud's relations, twelve in all,
Were very drunk at the judge's ball.

And when the summer came again,
The young bride bore him babies twain.

And the Judge was blest, but thought it strange
That bearing children made such a change:

For Maud grew broad and red and stout:
And the waist that his arm once clasped about

Was more than he now could span. And he
Sighed as he pondered, ruefully,

How that which in Maud was native grace
In Mrs Jenkins was out of place;

And thought of the twins, and wished that they
Looked less like the man who raked the hay

On Müller's farm, and dreamed with pain
Of the day he wandered down the lane.

And looking down that dreary track,
He half regretted that he came back.

For, had he waited, he might have wed
Some maiden fair and thoroughbred;

For there be women fair as she,
Whose verbs and nouns do more agree.

Alas for maiden! alas for judge!
And the sentimental, – that's one-half 'fudge';

For Maud soon thought the judge a bore,
With all his learning and all his lore.

And the judge would have bartered Maud's fair face
For more refinement and social grace.

If, of all words of tongue and pen,
The saddest are, 'It might have been,'

More sad are these we daily see:
'It is, but hadn't ought to be.'

FRANCIS BRET HARTE

The Heathen Pass-Ee

IN IMITATION OF BRET HARTE

Which I wish to remark,
    And my language is plain,
That for plots that are dark
    And not always in vain,
The heathen Pass-ee is peculiar,
    And the same I would rise to explain.

I would also premise
　　That the term of Pass-ee
Most fitly applies,
　　As you probably see,
To one whose vocation is passing
　　The 'Ordinary B.A. degree'.

Tom Crib was his name.
　　And I shall not deny
In regard to the same
　　What the name might imply,
But his face it was trustful and childlike,
　　And he had the most innocent eye.

Upon April the First
　　The Little-Go fell,
And that was the worst
　　Of the gentleman's sell,
For he fooled the Examining Body
　　In a way I'm reluctant to tell.

The candidates came
　　And Tom Crib soon appeared;
It was Euclid. The same
　　Was 'the subject he feared',
But he smiled as he sat by the table
　　With a smile that was wary and weird.

Yet he did what he could,
　　And the papers he showed
Were remarkably good,
　　And his countenance glowed
With pride when I met him soon after
　　As he walked down the Trumpington Road.

We did not find him out,
    Which I bitterly grieve,
For I've not the least doubt
    That he'd placed up his sleeve
Mr Todhunter's excellent Euclid,
    The same with intent to deceive.

But I shall not forget
    How the next day at two
A stiff paper was set
    By Examiner U ...
On Euripides' tragedy, Bacchae.
    A subject Tom 'partially knew'.

But the knowledge displayed
    By that heathen Pass-ee,
And the answers he made
    Were quite frightful to see,
For he rapidly floored the whole paper
    By about twenty minutes to three.

Then I looked up at U ...
    And he gazed upon me.
I observed, 'This won't do.'
    He replied, 'Goodness me!'
We are fooled by this artful young person,'
    And he sent for that heathen Pass-ee.

The scene that ensued
    Was disgraceful to view,
For the floor it was strewed
    With a tolerable few
Of the 'tips' that Tom Crib had been hiding
    For the 'subject he partially knew'.

On the cuff of his shirt
    He had managed to get

What we hoped had been dirt,
    But which proved, I regret,
To be notes on the rise of the Drama,
    A question invariably set.

In his various coats
    We proceeded to seek,
Where we found sundry notes
    And – with sorrow I speak –
One of Bohn's publications, so useful
    To the student of Latin or Greek.

In the crown of his cap
    Were the Furies and Fates,
And a delicate map
    Of the Dorian States,
And we found in his palms which were hollow,
    What are frequent in palms, – that is dates.

Which is why I remark,
    And my language is plain,
That for plots that are dark
    And not always in vain,
The heathen Pass-ee is peculiar,
    Which the same I am free to maintain.

A. C. HILTON

The Raven Replies to Poe

Charnel-minded Edgar Allan, surely you are nodding, shall an
Architect in planning put a lamp so far above the floor
As to shine down on a raven who has found a shaky haven
On the summit of a graven image higher than the door –
As to be above a bird above a bust above a door?
    They'd employ him nevermore!

It must make you even madder, Edgar, standing on your ladder,
When a visitor comes roaring in and flings you to the floor.
With your oil-can or your taper, you must cut a comic caper –
He'll suspect you are a japer lodging something on the door!
Oh, it's silly, Edgar, surely putting *props* above a door!
  Do not do it evermore!

                                                    J. A. LINDON

Alfred Lord Tennyson Forgets to Press Button B

'Button B. coins belong to P.M.G.' – Daily Paper

xxviii

I seized the dark machine, and spun
    With trembling hand the circle round,
    And listen'd; neither word nor sound
Was heard from Temple one two one.

Save, in the dark, a ghostly bell
    That echoed through the void of space,
    And measur'd, in that far-off place,
The beat of some vain sentinel.

You spoke not; in the mystic wire
    Nor wave, nor answering motion stirred;
    Within your silent room I heard
No voice to still my strong desire.

Shall we, I mused in sad despair,
    Who had sweet converse each with each
    And join'd in dear, familiar speech
Be sunder'd by the vacant air?

A keener sorrow fell; to me
    A sharper pain, beyond redress;
    Unthinking, I forgot to press
The secret spring of Button B.

Yet, if my wasted pledge should fall
    To him who rules both wire and post,
    'Tis better to have rung and lost
Than never to have rung at all.

G. H. VALLINS

In the Schools at Oxford

Butcher boys shouted without,
    – Within was writing for thee,
Shadows of three live men
    Talked as they walked into me,
Shadows of three live men and you were one of the three.

Butcher boys sang in the streets,
    The Bobby was far away,
Butcher boys shouted and sang
    In their usual maddening way.
Still in the Schools quite courteous you were torturing men all the
    day.

Two dead men I have known
    Examiners settled by me,
Two dead men I have scored,
    Now I will settle with thee.
Three dead men must I score, and thou art the last of the three.

ANON.

Disenchantment

He thought he saw Utopia
    As neatly planned as chess:
He looked again and saw it was
    Ubiquitous duress:
This does not gratify, he said,
    My bourgeois consciousness.

He thought he saw the truth of life
    As sex all unalloyed:
He looked again and saw it was
    A yarn of Sigmund Freud:
If this sprang from the *id*, he said,
    Its arguments are void.

He thought he saw full many a gem
    Of purest ray serene:
He looked again and saw it was
    A dose of Mescalin:
The price of visions is, he said,
    The headaches in between.

He thought he saw the Holy Ghost
    Lamenting in a mist:
He looked again and saw it was
    An existentialist:
It may be that he's right, he said,
    But what a pessimist.

He thought he saw some golden boys
    Our phoney world condemn:
He looked again and saw it was
    Some pimply A.Y.M.:
A dose of Epsom Salts, he said,
    Would ease the strain for them.

He thought he saw a projectile
    Descending from a height;
To blow the human race to bits
    And blast it out of sight:
He looked again and saw that he
    Was absolutely right.

KENNETH LILLINGTON

Omar for Housewives

Tomorrow a new Cook will come, you say,
To substitute the Cook of yesterday?
    But shall the summer day that brings the rose
Take Barbara and Mary Jane away?

I sometimes think that never burns the Bread
So black as when the tea is boiling red;
    That every cabbage plant the garden wears
Knows more than any human Cabbage-head.

And this new maid who looks so fresh and green,
On whom with all my woes I fain would lean;
    Ah, lean upon her lightly, for who knows
How soon she will get up and quit the scene?

Ah? my new handmaid! fill the pan that clears
Today of unwashed dishes, stacked in tiers.
    Tomorrow? Why, tomorrow I may be
Myself obliged to wash them – and for years!

Whether we roll in gold or have to pinch,
Whether the heart despair or merely flinch,
    The window panes grow speckier hour by hour,
The parlour dust is thickening inch by inch.

Well I remember, watching on a day
Sue handling china in a heartless way,
    Till one white teacup raised a broken rim
And murmured, 'Gently, Susan, gently pray!'

A box of biscuits underneath a Bough,
A can of beans, a bag of salt, and thou
    Burned out and singing in the wilderness.
Ah, wilderness were Paradise enow!

So when the Angel of the muddy drink,
Called coffee, throws the grounds into the sink,
    And, taking her departure, leaves you there
Alone to clean things up, you must not shrink;

But make the best of so-called 'Help', my friend,
Until we too into the dust descend.
    Take up the work where hirelings left it off,
Sans Hope, sans Help, sans Dishcloth – and sans end.

ANON.

An Unexpected Pleasure

My heart is like one asked to dine
    Whose evening dress is up the spout;
My heart is like a man would be
    Whose raging tooth is half pulled out.
My heart is like a howling swell
    Who boggles on his upper C;
My heart is madder than all these –
    My wife's mamma has come to tea.

Raise me a bump upon my crown,
    Bang it till green in purple dies;
Feed me on bombs and fulminates,
    And turncocks of a medium size.

Work me a suit in crimson apes
   And sky-blue beetles on the spree;
Because the mother of my wife
   Has come – and means to stay with me.

ANON.

Octopus

IN IMITATION OF SWINBURNE

Strange beauty, eight-limbed and eight-handed,
   Whence camest to dazzle our eyes?
With thy bosom bespangled and banded
   With the hues of the seas and the skies;
Is thy home European or Asian,
   O mystical monster marine?
Part molluscous and partly crustacean,
   Betwixt and between.

Wast thou born to the sound of sea-trumpets?
   Hast thou eaten and drunk to excess
Of the sponges – thy muffins and crumpets,
   Of the seaweed – thy mustard and cress?
Wast thou nurtured in caverns of coral,
   Remote from reproof or restraint?
Art thou innocent, art thou immoral,
   Sinburnian or Saint?

Lithe limbs, curling free, as a creeper
   That creeps in a desolate place,
To enrol and envelop the sleeper
   In a silent and stealthy embrace,
Cruel beak craning forward to bite us,
   Our juices to drain and to drink,
Or to whelm us in waves of Cocytus,
   Indelible ink!

O breast, that 'twere rapture to writhe on!
    O arms 'twere delicious to feel
Clinging close with the crush of the Python,
    When she maketh her murderous meal!
In thy eight-fold embraces enfolden,
    Let our empty existence escape;
Give us death that is glorious and golden,
    Crushed all out of shape!

Ah! thy red lips, lascivious and luscious,
    With death in their amorous kiss!
Cling round us, and clasp us, and crush us,
    With bitings of agonized bliss;
We are sick with the poison of pleasure,
    Dispense us the potion of pain;
Ope thy mouth to its uttermost measure
    And bite us again!

A. C. HILTON

My *Garden*

WITH A STERN LOOK AT T. E. BROWN

A garden is a *lovesome* thing? What rot!
Weed plot,
Scum pool,
Old pot,
Snail-shiny stool
In pieces; yet the fool
Contends that snails are not –
Not snails! in gardens! when the eve is cool?
Nay, but I see their trails!
'Tis very sure *my* garden's full of snails!

J. A. LINDON

They and We

With stormy joy the elephant
    Will bolt a thousand buns;
The cassowary grim and gaunt
    Will swallow stones by tons;
Man only, after dining out,
    By intermittent throes,
Either in fingers finds the gout
    Or finds it in his toes.

HORATIO SMITH

Jack and Jill

Here is the tale – and you must make the most of it!
    Here is the rhyme – ah, listen and attend!
Backwards – forwards – read it all and boast of it
    If you are anything the wiser in the end!

Now Jack looked up – it was time to sup, and the bucket was yet
    to fill,
And Jack looked round for a space and frowned, then beckoned his
    sister Jill,
And twice he pulled his sister's hair, and thrice he smote her side;
'Ha' done, ha' done with your impudent fun – ha' done with your
    games!' she cried;

'You have made mud pies of a marvellous size – finger and face are
    black,
You have trodden the Way of the Mire and the Clay – now up and
    wash you, Jack!
Or else, or ever we reach our home, there waiteth an angry dame –
Well you know the weight of her blow – the supperless open shame!
Wash, if you will, on yonder hill – wash, if you will, at the spring, –
Or keep your dirt, to your certain hurt, and an imminent walloping!'

'You must wash – you must scrub – you must scrape!' growled Jack,
    'you must traffic with cans and pails,
Nor keep the spoil of the good brown soil in the rim of your finger-
    nails!
The morning path you must tread to your bath – you must wash
    ere the night descends,
And all for the cause of conventional laws and the soap-makers'
    dividends!
But if 'tis sooth that our meal in truth depends on our washing, Jill,
By the sacred light of our appetite – haste – haste to the top of the
    hill!'

They have trodden the Way of the Mire and Clay, they have toiled
    and travelled far,
They have climbed to the brow of the hill-top now, where the
    bubbling fountains are,
They have taken the bucket and filled it up – yea, filled it to the
    brim;
But Jack, he sneered at his sister Jill, and Jill she sneered at him:
'What, blown already!' Jack cried out (and his was a biting mirth!)
'You boast indeed of your wonderful speed – but what is the
    boasting worth?
Now if you can run as the antelope runs, and if you can turn like a
    hare,
Come, race me, Jill, to the foot of the hill – and prove your boasting
    fair!'

'Race? What is a race' (and a mocking face had Jill as she spoke the
    word)
'Unless for a prize the runner tries? The truth indeed ye heard,
For I can run as the antelope runs, and I can turn like the hare:
The first one down wins half-a-crown – and I will race you there!'
'Yea, if for the lesson that you will learn (the lesson of humbled
    pride)
The price you fix at two-and-six, it shall not be denied;

Come, take your stand at my right hand, for here is the mark we
    toe:
Now, are you ready, and are you steady? Gird up your petticoats!
    Go!'

And Jill she ran like a winging bolt, a bolt from the bow released,
But Jack like a stream of the lightning gleam, with its pathway
    duly greased;
He ran down hill in front of Jill like a summer lightning flash –
Till he suddenly tripped on a stone, or slipped, and fell to the
    earth with a crash.
Then straight did rise on his wondering eyes the constellations fair,
Arcturus and the Pleiades, the Greater and Lesser Bear,
The swirling rain of a comet's train he saw, as he swiftly fell –
And Jill came tumbling after him with a loud triumphant yell:
'You have won, you have won, the race is done! And as for the
    wager laid –
You have fallen down with a broken crown – the half-crown debt is
    paid!'

They have taken Jack to the room at the back where the family
    medicines are,
And he lies in bed with a broken head in a halo of vinegar;
While, in that Jill had laughed her fill as her brother fell to earth,
She has felt the sting of a walloping – she hath paid the price of her
    mirth!

Here is the tale – and now you have the whole of it,
  Here is the story – well and wisely planned,
Beauty – Duty – these make up the soul of it –
  But, ah, my little readers, will you mark and understand?

ANTHONY C. DEANE

Thoughts at 8.5 a.m.

Oh often have I risen and shaved,
Yet hairy down at night have lain;
My beard despised the rest I craved.
See now, the fields with light are laved;
The sun streams through the window-pane;
And I must shave again.

Thus men themselves vain labours give;
Come, soap and brush – confound it, no!
Why still enact the Danaan sieve,
Or lather hours when I might live?
Into the gaping world I'll go,
And let the damned thing grow.

A. Y. CAMPBELL

A London Sparrow's

IF –

If you c'n keep alive when li'l bleeders
   Come arter y' wi' catapults an' stones;
If you c'n grow up unpertickler feeders,
   An' live on rubbidge, crumbs, an' 'addock bones;
If you c'n nest up in the bloomin' gutters,
   An' dodge the blinkin' tabby on the tiles;
Nip under wheels an' never git the flutters,
   Wear brahn an' no bright-coloured fevver-styles;
If you ain't blown b' nippers (Cor, I'd skin 'em!);
   Stop in y'r shells nah, warm-like, under me;
Yours is the eggs an' everyfink 'at's in 'em –
   An' when they 'atch, yor be cock-sparrers, see?

J. A. LINDON

Sweeney in Articulo

THE VOICE OF SWEENEY

Sunday is the dullest day, treating
Laughter as a profane sound, mixing
Worship and despair, killing
New thought with dead forms.
Weekdays give us hope, tempering
Work with reviving play, promising
A future life within this one.
Thirst overtook us, conjured up by Budweisserbräu
On a neon sign: we counted our dollar bills.
Then out into the night air, into Maloney's Bar.
And drank whiskey, and yarned by the hour.
Das Herz ist gestorben,* swell dame, echt Bronx.
And when we were out on bail, staying with the Dalai Lama,
My uncle, he gave me a ride on a yak,
And I was speechless. He said, Mamie,
Mamie, grasp his ears. And off we went
Beyond Yonkers, then I felt safe.
I drink most of the year and then I have a Vichy.

Where do we go from here, where do we go,
Out of the broken bottles? Pious sot!
You have no guide or clue for you know only
Puce snakes and violet mastodons, where the brain beats,
And a seltzer is no answer, a vomit no relief,
And the parched tongue no feel of water. Only
There is balm in this YMCA
(Claim now the balm inside the YMCA),
And you will see that there is more in life than
Those vigils at the doors of pubs in the morning,
Or bootings from the doors of pubs at closing time.

* Schiller, *Des Mädchens Klage.*

I will show you fear in a pile of half-bricks.
  Wer reitet so spät
  Durch Nacht und Wind?
  *Es ist der Vater mit seinem Kind.**

'You called me "Baby Doll" a year ago;
You said that I was very nice to know,'
But when we came back late from that Wimbledon dance-hall,
Your arms limp, your hair awry, you could not
Speak, and I likewise, we were neither
Living nor dead, and we knew nothing,
Gazing blankly before us in the carriage.
'Bank Station! All change! *Heraus! Heraus!*'

                                        VICTOR PURCELL

          advertisement
          in the style of
          e. e. cummings

       buy it from us kiddo
       you'll find it
       PAYS
       (and they last longer fit
       tit tit
       ting perfectly
       round the ribs waist back thighs
       etcetera)
       to purchase a
            BELLIMAN'S
              PELVO-BRA
                      (

       * Goethe, *Erlkönig.*

If It Buttons Beneath
etcetera
It Isn't A Belliman, Wear
One On The Beach

)

        SSIÈRE

giving medically approved

   U   R

   S PPO T

to your — and especially
if you have a

   S   N   T

     A I G S

      GG   BU

which of course you have
NOT –
etcetera

BELLIMAN'S BODYWEAR IS BEST

J. A. LINDON

Betjeman, 1984

I saw him in the Airstrip Gardens
   (Fahrenheit at 451)
Feeding automative orchids
   With a little plastic bun,
While above his brickwork cranium
   Burned the trapped and troubled sun.

'Where is Piper? Where is Pontefract?
   (Devil take my boiling pate!)
Where is Pam? And where's Myfanwy?
   Don't remind me of the date!

Can it be that I am *really*
  Knocking on for 78?

'In my splendid State Apartment
  Underneath a secret lock
Finger now forbidden treasures
  (Pray for me St Enodoc!):
T.V. plate and concrete lamp-post
  And a single nylon sock.

'Take your ease, pale-haired admirer,
  As I, half the century saner,
Pour a vintage Mazawattee
  Through the Marks and Spencer strainer
In a *genuine* British Railways
  (Luton Made) cardboard container.

'Though they say my verse-compulsion
  Lacks an interstellar drive,
Reading Beverley and Daphne
  Keeps *my* sense of words alive.
Lord, but *how* much beauty was there
  Back in 1955!'

CHARLES CAUSLEY

BITS AND PIECES

In Memoriam

Here lie the bones of Tammy Messer,
Of tarry woo' he was a dresser;
He had some faults and mony merits
And died of drinking ardent sperrits.

*

Here lies a woman, no man can deny it,
Who rests in peace although she lived unquiet,
Her husband prays you, if by her grave you walk
You gently tread, for if she wake she'll talk.

*

Here lies, cut down like unripe fruit,
The wife of Deacon Amos Shute.
She died of drinking too much coffee,
Anny Dominy, eighteen forty.

(FROM CONNECTICUT)

*

Here lies Bill Dodge
Who dodged all good
And dodged a deal of evil,
But after dodging all he could
He could not dodge the Devil.

*

Reader, pass on! – don't waste your time
On bad biography and bitter rhyme;
For what I am, this cumbrous clay insures,
And what I was is no affair of yours.

*

Within this grave do lie,
Back to back, my wife and I;
When the last trump the air shall fill,
If she gets up, I'll just lie still.

*

Beneath this plain pine board is lying
   The body of Joshua Hight,
'Cheer up,' the parson told him, dying;
   'Your future's very bright.'

Slowly the sick man raised his head,
   His weeping friends amazing.
'Parson, it's most too bright,' he said,
   'For I can see it blazing!'

(AMERICAN)

*

Here lies Stephen Rumbold
He lived to the age of an hundred and one
   Sanguine and strong
A hundred to one you don't live so long.

(FROM OXFORDSHIRE)

ON MR QUIRK, A LAWYER

Here lies Mr Quirk.
Still at the old work!

J. S. DRENNAN

Here lies the mother of children seven,
Four on earth and three in Heaven.
The three in Heaven preferring rather
To be with Mother than stay with Father.

(FROM NEAR CHICHESTER)

*

Alas friend Joseph
His death was almost sudden
As tho' the mandate came
    Direct from Heaven
His foot did slip and he did fall
Help help he cried and that was all

(FROM MYLOR CHURCHYARD, NEAR FALMOUTH)

*

Here lies the body of Mary Charlotte,
Born a virgin, died a harlot.
Until fifteen she kept her virginity,
Which is a record for this vicinity.

*

Poor Martha Snell, she's gone away,
She would if she could, but she couldn't stay;
She'd two bad legs and a baddish cough,
But her legs it was that carried her off.

*

Here lies one who for medicine would not give
A little gold, and so his life he lost:
I fancy now he'd wish again to live
Could he but guess how much his funeral cost.

*

Underneath this ancient pew
Lie the remains of Johnny Blue;
His name was Black, but that wouldn't do.

*

The manner of her death was thus:
She was druv over by a bus.

Cornish Toast

Here's to the Devil with his spade and wooden shovel
Digging tin by the bushel with his tail cocked up;

Here's to the Devil with his spade and wooden shovel
Digging taties by the bushel with his nightcap on.

'Yellow-Belly, Yellow-Belly, come for a swim' –
'Yes, by golly, when the tide comes in!'

ANON.

We are but Phantoms come and gone
Within a night's repose;
We've progressed ever on and on,
We are but Phantoms come and gone,
There is no sign in Wincanton
That anybody knows:
We are but Phantoms come and gone
Within a night's repose.

RACHEL ATTWATER (aged 13)

Pin your suspender-band tight;
And flee away into the blackness of the night!

S. ATTWATER (aged 6)

'Parding, Mrs Harding,
Is my kitting in your kitching garding,
Gnawing of a mutting-bone?'
'No, he's gone to Londing.'
'How many miles to Londing?
Eleving? I thought it was only seving.
Heavings! what a long way from home!'

ANON.

Eighteenth-Century Epigrams

I have lost my mistress, horse, and wife,
And when I think of human life,
    Cry mercy 'twas no worse.
My mistress sickly, poor and old,
My wife dam'd ugly and a scold, –
    I am sorry for my horse.

ANON.

'My dear, what makes you always yawn?'
The wife exclaimed, her temper gone;
    'Is home so dull and dreary?'
'Not so, my love,' he said, 'not so;
But man and wife are one, you know,
    And when alone I'm weary.'

ANON.

When Pontius wished an edict might be passed
That cuckolds should into the sea be cast,
His wife, assenting, thus replied to him:
'But first, my dear, I'd have you learn to swim.'

MATTHEW PRIOR (?)

These panting damsels, dancing for their lives,
Are only maidens waltzing into wives.
Those smiling matrons are appraisers sly,
Who regulate the dance, the squeeze, the sigh,
And each base cheapening buyer having chid,
Knock down their daughters to the noblest bid.

ANON.

How wisely Nature, ordering all below,
Forbade on woman's face the hair to grow.
For how could she be shaved, whate'er the barber's skill,
Whose tongue would never let her chin be still.

ANON.

THE BOOKWORMS

Through and through the inspirèd leaves,
Ye maggots, make your windings;
But oh! respect his lordship's taste,
And spare his golden bindings!

ROBERT BURNS

ADDRESSED TO A GENTLEMAN AT TABLE

WHO KEPT BOASTING OF THE COMPANY HE KEPT

What of lords with whom you've supped,
    And of dukes that you dined with yestreen!
A louse, sir, is still but a louse,
    Though it crawl on the locks of a queen.

ROBERT BURNS

FROM THE FRENCH

Aegle, beauty and poet, has two little crimes;
She makes her own face, and does not make her rhymes.

LORD BYRON

THE CASUIST

When Sarah Jane, the moral miss,
Declares 'tis very wrong to kiss,
   I'll bet a shilling I see through it:
The damsel, fairly understood,
Feels just as any Christian should –
   She'd rather suffer wrong than do it.

J. G. SAXE

ON THOMAS MOORE'S POEMS

Lallah Rookh
Is a naughty book
By Tommy Moore,
Who has written four,
Each warmer
Than the former.
So the most recent
Is the least decent.

SAMUEL ROGERS

My Bishop's eyes I've never seen
Though the light in them may shine;
For when he prays he closes his,
And when he preaches, mine.

ANON.

The house where once a lawyer dwelt
    Is now a smith's. Alas!
How rapidly the iron age
    Succeeds the age of brass!

WILLIAM ERSKINE

One Good Turn Deserves Another

A poor man went to hang himself,
    But treasure chanced to find;
He pocketed the miser's pelf
    And left the rope behind.

His money gone, the miser hung
    Himself in sheer despair:
Thus each the other's wants supplied,
    And that was surely fair.

ANON.

A Crime

On the first of September, one Sunday morn,
I shot a hen pheasant in standing corn
Without a licence. Contrive who can
Such a cluster of crimes against God and man!

LORD HOUGHTON

A Toast

Here's to a temperance supper,
    With water in glasses tall,
And coffee and tea to end with -
    And me not there at all!

ANON.

Cautionary Rhyme

After the rise, the fall:
  After the boom, the slump:
After the fizz and the fat cigar,
  The cigarette and the hump.

ANON.

Smiling Villain

Forth from his den to steal he stole,
His bags of chink he chunk,
And many a wicked smile he smole,
And many a wink he wunk.

ANON.

Predestination

We are the precious chosen few:
  Let all the rest be damned.
There's only room for one or two:
  We can't have Heaven crammed.

ANON.

Parson among the Pigeons

St Francis fed pigeons whenever he see 'em,
  But I saw a parson today
Who sat on the steps of the British Museum
  And frightened the pigeons away.

GEORGE MORROW

Lord High-Bo

Lord High-bo, getting tired of trains,
Would binge about in Aero-planes,
A habit which would not have got
Him into trouble, had he not
Neglected what we know to be
The rule of common courtesy.
Past bedroom windows he would sail
And with a most offensive hail
Disturb the privacy of those
About to wash or change their clothes.

HILAIRE BELLOC

Commonplace Verse

Behold the snowy mountains high
That stand against the azure sky,
The poplars waving in the breeze,
Also the Bloody-minded seas.

HILAIRE BELLOC

The Game of Cricket

I wish you'd speak to Mary, Nurse,
She's really getting worse and worse.
Just now when Tommy gave her out
She cried and then began to pout
And then she tried to take the ball
Although she cannot bowl at all.
And now she's standing on the pitch,
The miserable little Bitch!

HILAIRE BELLOC

Grandmamma's Birthday

Dear Grandmamma, with what we give,
We humbly pray that you may live
For many, many happy years:
Although you bore us all to tears.

HILAIRE BELLOC

Quiet Fun

My son Augustus, in the street, one day,
    Was feeling quite exceptionally merry.
A stranger asked him: 'Can you tell me, pray,
    The quickest way to Brompton Cemetery?'
'The quickest way? You bet I can!' said Gus,
    And pushed the fellow underneath a bus.

*

Whatever people say about my son,
He does enjoy his little bit of fun.

HARRY GRAHAM

Indifference

When Grandmamma fell off the boat,
And couldn't swim (and wouldn't float),
Matilda just stood by and smiled.
I almost could have slapped the child.

HARRY GRAHAM

Billy

Billy, in one of his nice new sashes,
Fell in the fire and was burned to ashes;
Now, although the room grows chilly,
I haven't the heart to poke poor Billy.

HARRY GRAHAM

Late last night I slew my wife,
Stretched her on the parquet flooring.
I was loath to take her life,
But I had to stop her snoring.

HARRY GRAHAM

Horse Sense: a Triolet

Sir Alfred Munnings, P.R.A.,
Roundly condemns Matisse,
Who does not paint like (shall we say?)
Sir Alfred Munnings, P.R.A.,
In strong approval horses neigh:
Loud cackle human geese.
Sir Alfred Munnings, P.R.A.,
Roundly condemns Matisse.

ALLAN M. LAING

Reproach

You, Mister Belloc, thought it fine
To put one's faith in God and Wine;
You see the Pickle I am in,
Who put my faith in Men and Gin!

W. BRIDGES-ADAMS

Toiling, rejoicing, sorrowing,
So I my life conduct;
Each morning sees some job begun,
Each evening sees it chucked.

ANON.

Yorkshire Pudding

Let us call Yorkshire pudding
A fortunate blunder;
It's a sort of popover
That's tripped and popped under.

OGDEN NASH

Stag Night, Palaeolithic

Drink deep to Uncle Uglug,
That early heroic human,
The first to eat an oyster,
The first to marry a woman.

God's curse on him who murmurs
As the banquet waxes moister,
'Had he only eaten the woman,
Had he only married the oyster!'

OGDEN NASH

A Boy's Will is the Wind's Will?

Mr Longfellow spoke only part of the truth,
Though a fatherly poet of pre-eminent rank;
A girl's will is the twister's will.
It can drive a parent through a two-inch plank.

OGDEN NASH

Sigmund Freud

Who's afreud of the big bad dream?
Things are never what they seem;
Daddy's bowler, Auntie's thimbles,
Actually are shocking symbols.
Still, I think, a pig's a pig –
Ah, there, symbol-minded Sig!

OGDEN NASH

Etiquette

A propos d'étiquette,
Le bon Roi Édouard Sept
Disait souvent (et pas enrhumé, ajoutons),
'Revenons, Messieurs, à nos boutons.'

L. E. JONES

Death

If Death were truly conquered, there would be
Too many great-great-great-great aunts to see.

L. E. JONES

The University Match

A thousand vicars prayed for a dry wicket;
When God sent rain they felt it wasn't cricket.

L. E. JONES

Publicity

A friend of mine (well, not a friend:
I've only met him once or twice,
But he amuses me no end)
Has taken up unnatural vice.

Of course it doesn't worry me
(I've never been with him alone),
But since his line is poetry
I rather think he wants it known.

DANIEL GEORGE

Gay birds

Cuckoos lead Bohemian lives,
They fail as husbands and as wives,
And so they cynically disparage
Everybody else's marriage.

ANON.

Translations from the Chinese

EXCEPTIS EXCIPIENDIS

Partner, sidekick, pal, old friend of mine
(Cried Chancellor Mu Kow
Benign with Burgundy and cheese soufflé)
I trust you everything: life, fortune, fair repute. ....
But I noticed the swift anguish
With which he retrieved, when he dropped it,
His little red book of Telephone Numbers.

CHRISTOPHER MORLEY

HEGELIAN ANTITHESIS

When, as a child, I noticed
That coal and ice were always sold
By the same merchant
I first suspected
The irremediable duplicity of the world.

CHRISTOPHER MORLEY

ANTHROPOMORPHIC

Even Jehovah
After Moses had got the Commandments
Committed to stone
Probably thought:
*I always forget the things
I really intended to say.*

CHRISTOPHER MORLEY

If all the trains at Clapham Jctn
Were suddenly to cease to fctn
The people waiting in the stn
Would never reach their destintn.

ANON.

Sapphics

Exquisite torment, dainty Mrs Hargreaves
Trips down the High Street, slaying hearts a-plenty;
Stricken and doomed are all who meet her eye-shots!
        Bar Mr Hargreaves.

Grocers a-tremble bash their brassy scales down,
Careless of weight and hacking cheese regardless;
Postmen shoot letters in the nearest ashcan,
      Dogs dance in circles.

Leaving their meters, gas-inspectors gallop,
Water Board men cease cutting off the water;
Florists are strewing inexpensive posies
      In Beauty's pathway.

'O cruel fair!' groan butchers at their chopping,
'Vive la belle Hargreaves!' howls a pallid milkman;
Even the Vicar shades his eyes and mutters:
      '*O dea certe.*'

Back to 'Balmoral' trips the goddess lightly;
Night comes at length, and Mr Hargreaves with it,
Casting his bowler glumly on the sideboard:
      'Gimme my dinner.'

D. B. WYNDHAM LEWIS

Efficiency Note

'She immediately retorted by biting a piece out of her lover's other ear.'
(Marseilles news-item)

Business-men on the Cannebière
Shrug and pass, having no time to spare;
   When a girl takes two very
   Hard bites at one chéri –
Alors, quoi? C'est pas ça, les affaires.

D. B. WYNDHAM LEWIS

From 'The Cruel Shepherdess'

'Rich women's knees
    Are sweet curiosities,
Their anfractuosities
    Dazzle and please.' –
Thus in the valley
    The shepherd-boy's song,
And naturally,
    The lad was wrong;
The hayseed erred;
    The young chawbacon
Was too absurd
    And quite mistaken:
The knobbliest trees
    Are more delightful;
Rich women's knees
    Are *simply frightful*.

D. B. WYNDHAM LEWIS

Grave Warning

(addressed, with the assistance of Daddy Wordsworth,
to a Too-Playful Débutante in a smart Night-Club)

'She shall be sportive as the fawn
That wild with glee across the lawn
    Or up the mountain springs'. . . .
But gentlemen were seen to yawn
At Lucy's games from dusk to dawn,
From boredom Strong Dislike was born,
    They started throwing things.

(Refrain, slow waltz-time):

'She was only a child of Nature,'
*   Said the Coroner, shaking his head,*
'But with all due regards to Her Majesty's Guards
*   There are times when a soldier sees red,*
*   Tra-la-la,*
*   There are times when a soldier sees red.'*

D. B. WYNDHAM LEWIS

Martial Remangled

I wonder not to see
    Your wife drink water:
But it amazes me
    That your wife's daughter
Drinks water.

JAMES BRIDIE

Superior people dub the Pig
A noisy, rude, disgruntled Whig;
But they're quite wrong about the boar – he
Is something *rasher* still: a Tory

K. MCDONAGH

Dumb Friends

I knew a poet who once loved a goat,
Than other poets' loves less boring, far;
For, though he often talked about its coat,
I never had to meet it in a bar.

ROBERT LIDDELL

Dead Sea Plage

Where once Lot's wife looked back in horror
To see God's judgement blast Gomorrah
Today the Sodom sunshine blisters
Queen Alexandra's Nursing Sisters.

ROBERT LIDDELL

Note on the Prevalence of Choristers

Nothing can glower
    Like a tourist throng
Trapped for an hour
    By Evensong.

PHYLLIS MCGINLEY

The Poet Sings the Passing of his Love

When Zoe's shop was simply labelled 'LUNCHES'
I took her roses every day in bunches.
But now she's changed it to 'YE LUNCHEON SHOPPE'
I've sent her one symbolic final poppe.

RICHARD USBORNE

Epitaph

('Is your bed attractive? Buy Quillettes.' – *Advertisement*)

Now Poppy Pentonville is dead,
It can, indeed it should, be said:
She had a most attractive bed.

RICHARD USBORNE

Henry Sutton

Henry Sutton
Made his wife
Serve him mutton
All his life.

When going to sleep,
His mind was rested
By counting the sheep
That he'd digested!

GERALD DEE

The Egotist

Himself is all he'll talk about to you,
A subject that, for him, has never cloyed,
Thus furnishing an unimpeded view
Into a vast, reverberating void.

H. A. C. EVANS

The Devil, having nothing else to do,
Went off to tempt the Inland Revenue;
The tax-collector, guessing it was he,
Devised a special form called Schedule D.
The Devil countered with a merry quip,
Since when the two have been in partnership.

BERNARD FERGUSSON

There once was a spinster of Bude
Who was such an incredible prude
That she got in a state o-
ver peeling potato
And serving it up in the nude.

ANON.

Epitaph

ON A PARTY GIRL

Lovely Pamela, who found
One sure way to get around,
Goes to bed beneath this stone
Early, sober, and alone.

RICHARD USBORNE

On Growing Old

I hope I'll not be hairless
There's nothing I could bear less.
Disease of the follicle
Is diabollicle!

I. KENVYN EVANS

The Louse

The louse
Has very little 'nous',
It's only pursuit
Is the hirsute.

I. KENVYN EVANS

National Types

Do not think it audacious
When Frenchmen embracious;
There is no economy
In their bonhomie.

No one would accuse the Greek
Of being meek.
The Persians at Thermopylae
Copped it properly,

The Yank
Is usually called 'Hank'
And has a nexus
With Texas.

I. KENVYN EVANS

Vive le Roi

Grief at the Loved One's parting from this Life
Is doubled for the ill-provided Wife.
With more Philosophy the Widow bears
That Husband's Loss who leaves behind some Shares.
Life's Continuity demands this so:
The Breadwinner is dead – long live the Dough!

JUSTIN RICHARDSON

Lineage

His Family was very Old,
Hers Older still, they used to boast;
Yet when their child was born, I'm told,
It seemed about as young as most.

JUSTIN RICHARDSON

Beggar on Horse-Power-Back

Where beggars wheedled, cadging hikers come,
And itching palm hands on to hitching thumb.
Small difference in the mendicants; each begs
Benevolence to spare his alms – or legs:
And Charity dispenses equal gifts –
Raising the lowly up, or giving lifts.

JUSTIN RICHARDSON

For the Record

His epigrams are not his own –
The man's an epigramaphone.

JUSTIN RICHARDSON

Homo Sap

Unlike wild duck I cannot fly,
Skeining the satin of the sky.
But I can do what they cannot –
Decoy them and then shoot the lot.

JUSTIN RICHARDSON

Limericks

There were once two young people of taste
Who were beautiful down to the waist;
    So they limited love
    To the regions above
And so remained perfectly chaste.

MONICA CURTIS

'For the tenth time, dull Daphnis,' said Chloe,
'You have told me my bosom is snoe
   And made pretty verse on
   Each part of my person –
Now do something, won't you, my boe?'

                VERA MEYNELL

There was a young lady of Ryde,
Who ate some green apples and died.
   The apples fermented
   Inside the lamented,
And made cider inside her inside.

                ANON.

There was a young lady of Bicester,
Who cried out when anyone kissed her,
   But a fellow named Ray
   Caught her out in this way.
He pretended, but then only missed her.

                ANON.

There was a young girl of Madras
Who had the most beautiful ass,
   But not as you'd think
   Firm, round, and pink,
But grey, with long ears, and eats grass.

                ANON.

Said a maid, 'I will marry for lucre,'
And her scandalized ma almost shucre.
   But when the chance came
   And she told the good dame,
I notice she didn't rebucre.

                ANON.

I wish that my room had a floor;
I don't care so much for a door,
    But this walking around
    Without touching the ground
Is getting to be such a bore.

GELETT BURGESS

There was a young lady of Tottenham,
Who'd no manners, or else she'd forgotten 'em;
    At tea at the vicar's
    She tore off her knickers
Because, she explained, she felt 'ot in 'em.

ANON.

There was an old man of Dunoon
Who always ate soup with a fork.
    For he said: 'As I eat
    Neither fish, fowl, nor flesh,
I should otherwise finish too quick.

ANON.

There once was a person from Lyme
Who married three wives at a time.
    When asked, 'Why a third?'
    He replied, 'One's absurd,
And bigamy, sir, is a crime.'

ANON.

When the French poodle saw in the hall
The great pool the umbrella let fall,
    He exclaimed, 'Ah, oui, oui,
    Now they'll all say it's me
For I always get blamed for it all.'

ANON.

HOME THOUGHTS FROM ABROAD

We were greatly impressed with the Dome –
So unlike dear St Peter's at home!
   Perhaps our church spire
   Is a tiny bit higher,
But our Vicar's much lower than Rome.

BRIAN HILL

AND FROM SOMEWHAT FURTHER

The alkaloid natives of Pollux
Engage in the strangest of frollux –
   They each get their kicks
   Chewing alkali sticks,
Which makes them, of course, alkihollux.

EDITH OGUTSCH

Five Clerihews

I am really rather annoyed
With Freud
For getting us all openly bumptious
About what had been secretly scrumptious.

One day Titian
Got into a somewhat equivocal position
When drawing from the nude.
She thought him just rude.

When Augustus John
Really did slap it on
His price was within 4d
Of Orpen's.

Henry Eight
Got up late.
Perhaps there was something to be said
For *his* staying in bed.

'Twas at Verona that Keats,
Finding strange company between the sheets,
To obviate future meetings
Invented Keatings.

EDMOND KAPP

And Five by the Master

'Dear me!' exclaimed Homer
'What a delicious aroma!
It smells as if a town
Was being burnt down.'

'Sire!' exclaimed Bossuet,
'You are behaving in a gross way.'
'Still, it's rather a lark,'
Replied the Grand Monarque.

It was a rule of Leonardo da Vinci's
Not to put his trust in princes.
Pleading was of no avail;
They had to pay up on the nail.

Chapman & Hall
Swore not at all.
Mr Chapman's yea was yea,
And Mr Hall's nay was nay.

Edward the Confessor
Slept under the dresser.
When that began to pall,
He slept in the hall.

E. C. BENTLEY

And Five More

Watteau
Was painting a nymph in a grotto.
He put up a notice 'Défense de Toucher'
To warn off Boucher.

I. GRIFFITH FAIRFAX

It is unfair
To be too hard on Hare.
Early anatomical work
Owes much to men like him and Burke.

AUTHOR UNKNOWN

Benjamin Disraeli
Wore a primrose daily.
This stimulated the phlegm
Of the G.O.M.

J. M. ROSS

Raymond Glendinning,
Though not quite sure what was winning,
Had definitely seen
That the course was wide and green.

MICHAEL SILLEY

Gilbert Scott
Might have been a lovesome thing, God wot,
If he had resisted the wiles
Of the manufacturers of encaustic tiles.

JOHN and ERNESTINE CARTER

Tut-Tut!

An oddity of Miss Dicker's
Was her readiness, behind the churchyard palings,
To take off her old-fashioned Vicar's
Principal failings.

J. A. LINDON

All Done by Mirrors!

Mrs Meek
Found a spot on her cheek.
Mrs Munt
Had more of a hunt.

J. A. LINDON

The Bride's First Cake

She whisked the eggs and sugar with a very solemn air;
The milk and butter also, and she took the greatest care
To add that little bit of baking powder which beginners often
    omit.
She mixed it all together and she baked it full an hour.
But never quite forgave herself for leaving out the FLOUR!

ANON.

The Higher Motive

The lower classes are such fools
They waste their money on the pools.
I bet, of course, but that's misleading.
One must encourage bloodstock breeding.

BERNARD FERGUSSON

Inhumanity

Man's inhumanity to man is hard,
In fact, 'tis scarce in line with aught that's human;
And yet – 'tis quite angelic as compared
With woman's inhumanity to woman.

ANON.

The old Feminist

Snugly upon the equal heights
    Enthroned at last where she belongs,
She takes no pleasure in her rights
    Who so enjoyed her wrongs.

PHYLLIS McGINLEY

Vive La France

You may sum
Up Madame;
And make pretty sure
Of Monsieur –
But you can never really tell
About mad damozel.

EDMOND KAPP

Garlic

Breakfast, dinner, supper, tea –
When'er Maria eats it;
In everything she says to me
She – so to speak – repeats it.

G. S. WHITTET

Clothes

When Eve, without leave, invented clothes,
Adam said: 'Madam, your fig-leaf shows.'

CLARK STILLMAN

Only men in rags
And gluttons old in sin
Treat their insides like carpet-bags
And shoot the victuals in.

ANON.

To a Lady

The enchantress Circe, with a potent wine,
Transformed her hapless lovers into swine;
But you, dear lady, it occurs to me,
Have not the slightest need of sorcery.

J. B. MORTON

Health and Fitness

Bruised by the masseur's final whack,
The patient lay without a sound;
Then, coming to, he hit him back.
Now masseur's in the cold, cold ground.

J. B. MORTON

An Old Gramophone Record

On the revolving disc her topmost note
    Pierced the loud music with a maniac yell,
As though a tiger had her by the throat.
    Il faut souffrir pour être Edison-Bell.

                    J. B. MORTON

'Lord Stanley of Alderley wishes in future to be known by the title of his
senior barony, Lord Sheffield.' – *The Times*

Trusty as steel, more valuable than plate,
Aspiring Sheffield knocked at Heaven's gate.
Top Man, who reads *The Times*, pronounced his doom,
Coldly remarking: 'Stanley, I presume?'

                    EVELYN WAUGH

Epitaph for a Would-be Poet

Here, 'beauty's victim' and 'cruel passion's prize',
For want of sublimating it he lies.
Too bad for him that he could not discov-
Er any less familiar rhymes for love.

                    ALAN BROWNJOHN

Last Trump

Here lies my love, the fair Ann Stidge,
Who died while playing a hand of bridge;
Game to the end, with Honours so,
Alas! 'twas spades that laid her low.

                    IVOR C. F. TREBY

The End of a Case-book

Tread carefully upon this hallowed spot,
For here a great detective's bones you'll find;
'Tis sad to think that such a simple Plot
Should overwhelm so very great a mind.

IVOR C. F. TREBY

On an Unsuccessful Diplomatist

Poor George, who failed at home when, as a youth,
He showed so great a disregard for truth,
Now fails abroad because, his youth gone by,
He can't remember how to tell a lie.

G. J. BLUNDELL

On a Modern Philosopher

Atheist once, he now with knowing nod
Proclaims himself on nodding terms with God.

G. J. BLUNDELL

On a Communist Cleric

This Marx the spot where, all serene,
    With Engels round his head,
His Reverence lies, in life so green,
    Although his sins were Red.

H. A. C. EVANS

After a Real Literary Dinner

'Who is the poet sitting in that chair
With rolling eyes and fiercely flaming hair?'
'Now, now, old boy, you really mustn't stare.
You recognize him, don't you?
He's not there!'

A. G. PRYS-JONES

Plain Murder

I saw a wasp upon a wall
And did not like his face at all:
And so the creature had no time
To wonder whether he liked mine.

A. G. PRYS-JONES

O (Modern) Helen!

The face that could have launched a thousand ships
And burnt the topless towers of Ilium
Is happy, now, to feast on fish and chips
With Harris, prior to the Odeon.

A. G. PRYS-JONES

Young Man of Porthcawl

There was a young man of Porthcawl
Who thought he was Samson or Saul:
These thoughts so obscure
Were due to the brewer,
And not to his ego at all.

A. G. PRYS-JONES

Tragic Hobby

An artist who lived at St Ives
Collected quaint African knives:
But his children all thought
They were bought for their sport:
Out of eight only one now survives.

A. G. PRYS-JONES

The Disillusioned Chemist

Her Breach of Promise action laid me low –
In black are my retorts and test-tubes clothed.
For what a lot of LsD_2O
At passion's death, $2NeXb$-trothed.

D. R. PEDDY

Epitaph on a Senior Civil Servant

Here lies Sir John; despite his fame
In departmental annals,
Death, when it notified its claim,
By-passed the proper channels.

D. R. PEDDY

Nuclear Trifle

The Spacemen of the Atom Age
    On their unearthly trips
Will feed their fissile faces on
    Atomic fission chips.

G. C. NORMAN

Book Talk

Poor Mr Graham Greene is greatly grieved.
He has to be obscene to be believed.

G. C. NORMAN

Central Eating

Radi was a circus lion,
Radi was a woman hater,
Radi had a lady trainer,
Radiator.

IVOR C. F. TREBY

At bedtime good girls all get hotties*
But naughty girls get smacks on botties.

ANON. (aged 6½)

* Hotwater bottle (Australian).

INDEX OF AUTHORS